Praise for *The Meaningful Middle School Classroom*

"*The Meaningful Middle School Classroom* is an essential read for every middle school educator and administrator! Jen expertly blends the research, her extensive classroom and professional experiences, and her passion for this work into every page. This book challenges and inspires us to keep elevating our practices for our worthy students."

—**Mary Gorr**, superintendent of
Mount Prospect School District 57

"This book equips educators with resources to spark joy, meaningful connections, and deep learning in middle schools. Drawing on research and her experience as an educator, Ciok offers concrete ways to foster student engagement and connect learning to the real world. A must-read for those dedicated to impactful middle level education."

—**Lisa M. Harrison**, PhD, dean and professor,
Patton College of Education, Ohio University

"*The Meaningful Middle School Classroom* shares stories from within the classroom that inspire and resonate. Each chapter centers on student experience and adolescent development. It highlights the importance of data collection and provides actionable ideas. This book reminds teachers that fostering meaning and connection in middle school isn't only necessary—it can also be magical."

—**Leticia Romero**, 7th and 8th grade ELA teacher

"This book is an essential resource for anyone working with young adolescents. Jennifer Ciok blends research and practice to highlight strategies that make learning engaging and relevant. It's filled with actionable ideas that help students ask questions, make meaning, and build connections in and beyond the classroom."

—**Abby Gillespie**, Youth-Nex, The University of Virginia Center to Promote Effective Youth Development

"Jennifer Ciok has grounded this text in love and whole student well-being. *The Meaningful Middle School Classroom* is a must-have for any middle school teacher or leader. It is such a wonderfully intentional guide to sparking engagement in students that will carry them their whole academic careers."

—**Rachel Parnell**, educator and equity champion

"Student engagement is a critical element of learning, especially in the middle grades and high school. Jennifer Ciok's advice on how to create authentic and exciting engagement in the classroom is not only based on solid research but also years of practical experience working with kids. Both veteran and novice classroom teachers will turn to the pages and pages of sample lessons and activities every time they sit down to plan for their classes. And instructional coaches and administrators will be better prepared to offer practical advice after reading this book."

—**Timothy Dohrer**, PhD, National Louis University

The Meaningful Middle School Classroom

The Meaningful Middle School Classroom

How to SPARK Engagement That Fosters Deep Learning

Jennifer K. Ciok

ascd

Arlington, Virginia USA

2111 Wilson Boulevard, Suite 300 • Arlington, VA 22201 USA
Phone: 800-933-2723 or 703-578-9600
Website: www.ascd.org • Email: member@ascd.org
Author guidelines: www.ascd.org/write

Richard Culatta, *Chief Executive Officer;* Anthony Rebora, *Chief Content Officer;* Genny Ostertag, *Managing Director, Book Acquisitions & Editing;* Susan Hills, *Senior Acquisitions Editor;* Mary Beth Nielsen, *Director, Book Editing;* Liz Wegner, *Editor;* Georgia Park, *Graphic Designer;* Valerie Younkin, *Senior Production Designer;* Kelly Marshall, *Production Manager;* Shajuan Martin, *E-Publishing Specialist*

Copyright © 2025 ASCD. All rights reserved. It is illegal to reproduce copies of this work in print or electronic format (including reproductions displayed on a secure intranet or stored in a retrieval system or other electronic storage device from which copies can be made or displayed) without the prior written permission of the publisher. By purchasing only authorized electronic or print editions and not participating in or encouraging piracy of copyrighted materials, you support the rights of authors and publishers. Readers who wish to reproduce or republish excerpts of this work in print or electronic format may do so for a small fee by contacting the Copyright Clearance Center (CCC), 222 Rosewood Dr., Danvers, MA 01923, USA (phone: 978-750-8400; fax: 978-646-8600; web: www.copyright.com). To inquire about site licensing options or any other reuse, contact ASCD Permissions at www.ascd.org/permissions or permissions@ascd.org. For a list of vendors authorized to license ASCD ebooks to institutions, see www.ascd.org/epubs. Send translation inquiries to translations@ascd.org.

ASCD® is a registered trademark of Association for Supervision and Curriculum Development. All other trademarks contained in this book are the property of, and reserved by, their respective owners, and are used for editorial and informational purposes only. No such use should be construed to imply sponsorship or endorsement of the book by the respective owners.

All web links in this book are correct as of the publication date below but may have become inactive or otherwise modified since that time. If you notice a deactivated or changed link, please email books@ascd.org with the words "Link Update" in the subject line. In your message, please specify the web link, the book title, and the page number on which the link appears.

PAPERBACK ISBN: 978-1-4166-3365-5   ASCD product #125008 n5/25
PDF EBOOK ISBN: 978-1-4166-3366-2; see Books in Print for other formats.

Quantity discounts are available: email programteam@ascd.org or call 800-933-2723, ext. 5773, or 703-575-5773. For desk copies, go to www.ascd.org/deskcopy.

Library of Congress Cataloging-in-Publication Data
Names: Ciok, Jennifer K author
Title: The meaningful middle school classroom : how to spark engagement that fosters deep learning / Jennifer K Ciok.
Description: Arlington, VA : ASCD, [2025] | Includes bibliographical references and index.
Identifiers: LCCN 2025000074 (print) | LCCN 2025000075 (ebook) | ISBN 9781416633655 paperback | ISBN 9781416633662 pdf | ISBN 9781416633679 epub
Subjects: LCSH: Middle school education | Motivation in education | Learning ability | Storytelling in education | Thought and thinking
Classification: LCC LB1623 .C48 2025 (print) | LCC LB1623 (ebook) | DDC 373.1102—dc23/eng/20250401
LC record available at https://lccn.loc.gov/2025000074
LC ebook record available at https://lccn.loc.gov/2025000075

34 33 32 31 30 29 28 27 26 25   1 2 3 4 5 6 7 8 9 10 11 12

*To all those who create spaces of joy where
every student feels seen, valued, and heard,
I see you and deeply appreciate your efforts.*

The Meaningful Middle School Classroom

Preface xi

1. The Adolescent Brain and the Quest to Find Meaning 1
2. Understanding Students' Thinking and Experiences:
   The Importance of Data 18
3. The Power of Storytelling 49
4. Integrating the Arts 77
5. Connecting Learning to Life Outside School 113
6. Finding the Spark Every Day 140
7. The Path Forward 156

Acknowledgments 173

References 175

Index 179

About the Author 185

Preface

Student, teacher, lead, partner, specialist, manager, facilitator, coach, school board member, advocate, parent—these are all titles and roles that I have held in the vast world of education, often two or three of them at the same time. I have been on all sides of the table, discussing students, curriculum, social-emotional health, accommodations, grades, attendance, mandates, and test scores. I understand how hard it is to balance all the competing interests and the tension that so many educators feel in the quest to ensure that their students have the best possible experience in school. I also know that in a time when education is more important than ever, it is vital to find that spark that ignites learning as we listen to, believe in, and engage students, especially those in the middle grades, in work that is meaningful and connected to their lives in and outside school.

Despite my experience in all the roles I have held, I know that there is a lot I don't know. With that in mind, I took a communal approach to writing this book by gathering voices of educators, researchers, coaches, and students from across the United States to include their expertise, experiences, and perspectives about what it means to engage middle school students and spark their curiosity. I am so incredibly grateful to the many people who sparked my own thinking, shared their brilliance, and helped me to give life to this book.

The Power of a Spark

What comes to mind when you think of a spark? For me, a spark is the moment when I could almost see the connections being made in my students' heads—the "ohhhhhh" moment when they saw the *how* and *why* behind what we were learning in class and how it connected to their world. It was the moment when a student excitedly ran into my classroom and told me that they had gone home and shared something we had done the day before with a family member or that they had continued to dig into a topic and had found some new fact, idea, or connection. Or even when, years down the road, a student would return and tell me how something we did in middle school had affected a decision they had made about what to be involved in at high school or college or even as they found their first job. These sparks often start small, with one day or one lesson, but quickly grow into a fire that fuels purpose and meaning.

How Can We Ignite a Spark in Students?

Throughout this book, I use quotes, examples from my colleagues, my own experiences, and research on adolescent development to explore different ways educators can use qualitative and quantitative data to build a curriculum and a classroom environment where students feel that spark and where they feel seen, valued, heard, and engaged. We will look at ways that students can begin to make meaningful connections to the work they are doing in school, which in turn will lead to greater engagement and better future outcomes. Each chapter includes things to think about before implementation and practical ways to use these strategies. At the end of every chapter, using the acronym SPARK (Study, Pilot, Analyze, Reflect, Kindle), there are reflection questions for things to consider as you incorporate some of these new ideas into your classroom (see Figure 0.1).

FIGURE 0.1
Finding the SPARK

Study—What formal and informal information are you collecting from your students? How can you involve your students in the process of gathering that information?

Pilot—What new ideas can you try in your classroom?

Analyze—What patterns and trends did you notice as you put new ideas into practice?

Reflect—What worked? How do you know? What should you continue to do? What changes can you make?

Kindle—How can you keep the spark going for your students and for yourself?

We begin in Chapter 1 with an explanation of the adolescent brain and how it experiences a period of development second only to that which occurs in the first years of childhood. New synapses are formed, strengthened, and stabilized, and others that aren't frequently used are pruned. Students begin to explore questions related to their identity and their place in the world. Their curiosity intensifies, and trust becomes a more critical element in their existing and developing relationships.

In Chapter 2, we dig into the ways that qualitative methods and surveys can be used to gather information to better understand how students are experiencing school and how they can be co-creators in making informed changes to their classrooms based on the findings. These practices help educators to investigate what students want and need before trying different strategies.

Chapter 3 looks at how educators can create experiences where students feel seen, valued, and heard using the students' own stories and backgrounds. As will be discussed in Chapter 1, students in middle school are very focused on who they are and how they fit in with their peers. What better way to support their search for identity than to include it in the curriculum? This chapter includes big and small ideas for how to implement this type of storytelling in a classroom.

Chapter 4 considers multiple ways to bring art into the classroom to express emotions and to foster students' curiosity and interest in their own community and the world, both past and present. Analyzing songs, photos, or artwork can help make a topic come alive while giving every student an entry point to the content, landmarks to connect their learning to, and opportunities to build stronger relationships with their classmates and the school community.

Chapter 5 explores the question that so many students ask: "How will I use this in the real world?" In my experience, much of what students remember from middle school are things that connect to their interests and goals or a time when they felt they made a lasting impact. This chapter looks at what students have said about how to bring relevancy into the classroom using real-world applications, passion projects, and service learning. From group work, to finding reliable sources, to outdoor education trips, so much of what sticks with students has to do with skills that will help them navigate the world around them—including their friendships, the adults in their lives, and the experiences they have at this pivotal point in their educational journey.

Chapter 6 discusses quick ways to infuse relevancy and meaning into the classroom each day through data collection, storytelling, art, and real-world experiences. Through these examples, including suggestions for daily or monthly themes, this chapter offers ideas for how to help your students make connections, share their thinking, and find the joy in learning.

And finally, in Chapter 7, we look at a path forward. Oftentimes digging into a topic leaves you with more questions than answers. Alongside reflections from educators, researchers, coaches, and other practitioners on the ever-evolving world of education, there are practical steps for how to add some of these ideas into your classroom, along with reflection questions and a checklist to help you get started.

1

The Adolescent Brain and the Quest to Find Meaning

We've just explained why adolescents are so frustrating, great, asinine, impulsive, inspiring, destructive, self-destructive, selfless, selfish, impossible, and world changing.

—Robert M. Sapolsky, *Behave: The Biology of Humans at Our Best and Worst*

It's a cold Tuesday morning in January. I'm standing in front of a class of 26 7th graders. We are getting ready to continue our study of worker and consumer rights in the late 1800s/early 1900s by reading a passage from Upton Sinclair's *The Jungle*. Considering we are in the suburbs of Chicago, about 20 miles from where the book is set, many of my students are very interested to see what this passage has to say about how workers were treated and what customers were buying. As an opening to the lesson, students in groups of three are discussing where food comes from and how they know it is safe to eat. As I'm watching them interact, I observe so many different things happening all at once. One student is excitedly sharing about a documentary she watched about this topic. I overhear her mention the Food and Drug Act and something about the difference between free-range chickens and caged chickens. Others are talking about our discussion in class the day before, including information about President Theodore Roosevelt and consumer protections. A few students are frantically flipping through their notes, trying to find the information that they want to share. Two students have their hands up. I walk over to find out what they need. One asks to use the restroom, and the other wants to have an in-depth conversation about the Food and Drug Administration (FDA). He asks if I believe the FDA is still effective and if I think there should be additional regulations on food dyes and preservatives. While engaging in that discussion, I also notice that some students have disengaged completely, their heads down, and a few others haven't said a word because, I believe, they are afraid they might say something wrong in front of their classmates. As the teacher, I'm watching in real time as students navigate their place in our classroom and how they engage with their peers, the content, and their own identity.

A Time of Continual Change

Who am I? Who am I in this community? Who am I in the world? These are questions that we all wrestle with in different ways. The answers shift and change as we learn more, experience more, and understand more about ourselves and the world around us. Think back to your own childhood. What did you think your life would look like when you were an adult? How did that notion shift in middle school? In high school? How about as you entered college or another postsecondary pathway? Have you remained at your first place of employment? Changed careers completely? Traveled somewhere that made you think differently? Met someone or had an experience that changed your outlook?

For students in middle school, these questions are constantly swirling as they navigate the changes in their bodies, their brains, and how they interact with their peers and the adults in their lives. For some students, these questions manifest as a curiosity for what is happening in the world around them and a constant wondering about how all the new things they are learning fit together. For others, these changes can lead to a feeling of anxiousness, which can in turn lead to avoiding risk taking or new situations. Other students may act out and disrupt environments where they feel unsure. And still others may float through, not seeming to worry about anything at all. And as all middle school educators know, students at this age can go from one extreme to another in a matter of minutes with very little warning. They may be extremely engaged in one class but completely disengaged in another. They may come back from lunch a totally different person than they were in the morning. And yet, as anyone who works with this age also knows, these students are truly an amazing group to work with and to learn from because they are constantly making new connections, learning new things, and speaking their truth in thoughtful and sometimes hilarious ways.

Researchers have found that young adolescence is the second window of opportunity for brain development. "In addition to body changes, the onset of puberty may trigger a second period of brain plasticity, increasing both the opportunity and vulnerability inherent in adolescence" (Harper et al., 2018, p. 5). This is a time when the brain goes through a critical cycle of brain development that is second only to the development that occurs in early childhood. At the age of 11 or 12, the neurons in the brain begin to form additional synapses. Then, throughout the remaining years of adolescence and based on a young person's experiences, those synapses that are used regularly are stabilized and strengthened, while those that are not are eliminated or "pruned" away. This reshaping is where the idea of "use it or lose it" comes from (Spinks, 2000). This time of growth and consolidation of learning also begins to explain why students in the middle grades are so invested in finding work that is meaningful to them, and how their brains are wired to engage in lessons, experiences, and projects that they find relevant to their own lives and their future.

Students at this age also spend a lot of time asking questions and trying to make meaning. Their inquisitiveness should be fostered through exploration and discovery; but, as noted by Jenny Nagaoka, the deputy director of the UChicago Consortium on School Research, middle school classrooms often become more structured and less open to flexibility and collaboration instead of being set up with the understanding that students are more capable of doing independent work or working in partnership with their classmates (personal communication, October 10, 2023). In middle school, there is often a lot of talk of teachers having to prepare students for high school or get them ready for the "real world" in order to explain the need to be more rigid and structured in the classroom. And though routine is vitally important so students know what to expect and what they need to do to be successful, that doesn't mean that the flexibility, creativity, collaboration, and joy that are sometimes more evident in the earlier grades should disappear.

"Who Am I?"

Identity formation happens in many ways throughout the middle school years. In 2023, Youth-Nex, a research center at the University of Virginia, put out a report titled *Portrait of a Thriving Youth*. It identified six key interconnected domains of adolescent learning and development: health, cognition, identity, meaning and purpose, emotion, and social. In their portrait, the authors defined the development of identity as discovering "who we are now and who we may be in the future" (Youth-Nex, 2023, p. 16). For students, this means they are continually shaping and reshaping their values, beliefs, and understanding of themselves and their relationships with friends and family. In these formative years, students are trying on different identities through their style, who they hang out with, their priorities, and how they show up in various spaces. They take on different roles in the classroom; some become the ones who answer every question, whereas others stay quiet and take in every word. Some aren't sure that school is for them, whereas others are continuing to search for something that grabs their interest.

For students, understanding who they are and the role they play is extremely important. As art teacher Meredith Kachel commented, "I think we all have different roles in life and having [students] figure that out organically instead of assigning it is really helpful.... Some kids are straight-up engineers, and they know exactly what they're going to do. And there are some kids who are more 'processy,' like makers who want to be hands-on" (personal communication, November 20, 2023). Giving students opportunities to try on different roles helps them to have new experiences that reshape their current thinking about who they are, what they can do, and who they eventually want to be.

The middle school years are one of the best times to foster that exploration. As Ashlee Sjogren, a research assistant professor from the University of Virginia, noted, the adolescent brain is exactly where it needs to be for this time in life, as adolescents are ripe for all the experiences they are having and their brain is malleable enough to be molded by those experiences (personal communication, October 20, 2023). The experimentation and exploration that occur will serve them well in the future, as they encounter and then have to navigate new circumstances, and so adolescence is a great time for joining new clubs, sports, or other activities in and outside school. Because students are becoming more curious about the world around them, it is also an opportune time for them to volunteer to help others and to learn about ways to support people in their own community and around the world. This is also the time when students become more independent, as they begin to wonder what the future might bring.

"Why Are We Doing This?"

Because students are becoming more curious in middle school, they often begin to question everything from *what* they are learning to *how* they are learning it. They are beginning to push back on the "because I told you to" line and are trying to understand more about the ways adults are thinking. Nagaoka explained it this way: "[Middle schoolers] ask questions, which may come off like questioning authority, but it's because they're trying to learn. They're trying to get what it is and why it is that adults are telling them or wanting them to do different things, or why they're acting in a certain way, which is something that's entirely new to them. So it's this whole new world of understanding the brains of other people, and they're just trying to figure it out" (personal communication, October 10, 2023). Knowing that this behavior is developmental can help teachers see this constant questioning as less of an annoyance or as students just wanting to be difficult and get out of work, and more of a situation in which students are being curious and wanting to better understand the *why* behind the work they are being asked to complete. Cathy Gormley, a middle school science teacher, often sees this play out in her classroom. She notes that "students questioning everything" is one of the things she loves about her job. She admits that "it can be a challenge at times, [but] when you think about it, it's really wonderful. I didn't see it as much at the start of my career as I do now. It's not questioning, 'Why are you like this?' It's wondering, 'How is this going to help me? How is this meaningful to me? What can I do with this information?' They are questions that I, as an adult, ask all the time. Their questioning, I think, is going to help them really decide what path is important to them, either as an individual or as a society, and it's pretty mature, to be honest" (personal communication, November 6, 2023).

Taking time in class to explain the *why* behind the work can make a big difference for middle school students. Many educators post the objective for their lessons somewhere in the classroom, and though this can be helpful, without explanation and connection, it is often intended more for the adults who come into the room than it is for the students. To answer the *why* question effectively, educators and students need to reflect together on how the content connects to other things students have learned, what skills they are gaining, and how this topic connects to their life outside school. It's important for educators to appeal to their students' current interests and curiosities. Getting students excited about this cool and interesting thing they are learning right now is often much more effective than sharing how it will help them with a far-off outcome like a career or a distant goal. Giving students time to ask questions about the *why* helps them to see themselves as part of the learning and as having agency instead of just having the curriculum "done" to them.

"Who Am I in This (School) Community?"

You often hear middle school students say that they aren't a "math person" or an "art person," or that reading or science isn't their "thing." The middle school years are a complex time academically and socially for students. If they haven't been successful in the past, they start to think that they are not good at certain skills, which sometimes causes them to be less likely to take risks when they fear that their classmates may make fun of them or that they may fail.

However, this is also a time when students can do a lot more than they could in the past. They can engage in more abstract thinking and in more complex curriculum and topics. As educators, we have to create spaces where students feel like they can take those risks and try new things. Risk taking is socially and psychologically transforming, and it "provides intense experiences from which adolescents construct stories of themselves and out of which meaningful bonds are forged" (Scanlon, 2024). Students' learning experiences and the environmental influences around them play key roles in their development. Learning and development are linked and affect the neural connections that are strengthened during adolescence (Harper et al., 2018).

When I asked improvement coaches Curtis Taylor and Yekaterina Milvidskaia what they thought was the most important thing for educators to know about adolescent brain development, they warned against "hijacking the amygdala," or causing the part of the brain that processes emotions to have a disproportionate response to the situation they are in. If the amygdala is hijacked, a student's defenses go up, and they end up in a fight, flight, or freeze mode. In a classroom, this situation can present as a student lashing out at a teacher or peer, shutting down and refusing to work, or even trying to escape to the bathroom or another safe space in the building. Triggers for this response may come from an interaction with peers, a conrontation with someone in authority, or a change in their own understanding of the world around them. Milvidskaia suggested that one way to prevent these triggers from hijacking a student's amygdala is to create academic safety in the classroom (personal communication, November 30, 2023). Taylor added, "Academic safety is a big thing in our practice of making sure that students feel welcomed, feel like they belong, and just feel safe in the classroom. Because if you are always in anxiety mode, you're not going to learn" (personal communication, November 30, 2023).

In the executive summary to the report *Teaching Adolescents to Become Learners* (Farrington et al., 2012a), the authors state, "We can create environments that support noncognitive development—schools and spaces where students feel their work is meaningful, where they know adults believe in their ability, and where they genuinely believe in their own capacity to learn, grow, and succeed" (p. 1). The authors identify the following four academic mindsets that affect student performance and that can be shaped by school and classroom contexts:

- I belong in this academic community.
- My ability and competence grow with my effort.
- I can succeed at this.
- This work has value for me. (Farrington et al., 2012b, p. 9)

As I think about how students interact with their communities, I often consider how they would react to those four statements and how they might respond to the following questions:

- Do they feel like they belong in the classroom, with their peers, and in the school as a whole? What does that look like and feel like for them? How can we as educators know?
- Do they think that their ability and knowledge are growing with the effort they are putting in? What can we as educators do to help reinforce that? What do we do that may stifle this mindset?
- Do they truly feel like they can succeed at the task in front of them? How do we respond when a student shuts down? What happens when they don't succeed on the first try (or the second or third)?
- Do they think their work has value or that it is valued by other people? What does meaningful work look like to a middle schooler? What type of work have they found value in in the past?

As educators, it is our job to establish classroom conditions to best support students so they don't feel threatened and so they know they can take risks in order to learn, grow, and succeed.

"Who Can I Trust?"

Along with positive learning conditions, forming trusting relationships is an integral part of the middle school experience. In her book *One Trusted Adult*, Brooklyn Raney (2019) explains how having a trusted adult "can significantly reduce risk, give you a safe place for processing normal life questions, provide a teacher and model of important life skills, and help you calibrate your inner compass" (p. xviii). Making sure that students feel they have someone they can go to at school, especially during this time of so much change in their lives, can have a genuine positive impact.

One way to do this is by intentionally matching students to an adult in the school with whom they already have a connection, or, for those who don't have such a connection, building that connection to a caring adult mentor in an authentic way. The most effective way I have done this is by using a modified relationship-mapping strategy informed by the protocol developed by the Making Caring Common project (Harvard Graduate School of Education, 2024). The strategy follows these four steps:

1. Have students identify, through a quick survey, a teacher they feel connected to. We defined *connection* as someone they would go to if they had a problem. If you want to have an even better understanding of why they chose that person, you can also have them briefly explain their choice or what that person has done to support them.
2. On a spreadsheet listing all the students, have teachers identify which students they feel would come to them with a problem. More than one teacher can identify a single student.
3. As a group, analyze the lists by looking first for those students who don't feel they have a connection to any adults. You should also flag any student no teachers identified as having a connection to, even if the student says they feel a connection.
4. At this point, go through the list and intentionally map students who have been flagged. Start with those who don't feel connected to any teacher, and map them to one of the teachers who said they feel like that student would come to them with a problem. If no teacher has identified

that particular student, then map the student to a teacher who believes they can build a solid relationship with that student. If no teachers felt a particular student would come to them with a problem but the student had, in fact, identified feeling a connection with a specific teacher, make sure that the teacher knows that the student trusts them and would come to them with a problem so they can continue to strengthen that relationship.

Once the matching is completed, teachers should check in with their smaller groups of students for a few minutes each day or as often as possible during the week. Those check-ins shouldn't be about grades or missing work but about the student as a person. It's helpful to take brief notes on what is learned, especially if it's something that is important for the student's other teachers to know. Share those notes at a team meeting or in another forum where you can talk about individual students and supports they may need.

After a couple of months, give the same survey again and see if the students who didn't originally feel a connection feel more supported and connected. You can also see if there are students who originally felt connected but experienced something that caused the connection to be lost.

The relationship-mapping strategy helps to build intentional connections, which for many students can make all the difference. Just knowing that someone would notice if they weren't there helps to keep them connected to school and to feel that their voice is valued in the community. During a time when students may feel isolated and technology can keep them from connecting in person, these intentional interactions can help them feel like they belong and help them to build skills for connecting with adults and peers in meaningful ways. Though the middle school years are an awkward time for everyone, students often feel like they are going through it alone. Helping them understand and name what they are feeling and giving them time and space to work through those emotions is an important part of working with middle school students.

"Who Am I in This World?"

The Search Institute defines *sparks* as "the interests and passions young people have that light a fire in their lives and express the essence of who they are and what they offer to the world" (Scales, 2010, p. 1). Through a series of surveys of 13,000 students in grades 5 through 12, the institute found that 66 percent of students said that they have at least one thing that is a spark for them, and 55 percent of that same group said that they had an adult who supported them in developing their spark. For many students, that spark is what makes them excited to come to school each day and keeps them motivated. It's what allows them to take risks, make new friends, and thrive at school.

As teachers, we can help to foster these sparks by providing diverse developmental experiences, listening to students, and giving them time to explore and try new roles and activities. In the study *Adolescent Thriving: The Role of Sparks, Relationships, and Empowerment,* the authors (Scales et al., 2010) identified six questions to ask students regarding their spark:

1. What is your spark?
2. When and where do you express it?
3. Who knows your spark?
4. Who nourishes your spark?
5. What gets in your way?
6. How can I help you find and keep your spark?

What I love about these questions is that they are open-ended and nonjudgmental. They can foster a conversation that allows for dreaming and for realistic problem solving. Some students will be able to answer them immediately, whereas others may not and then come back days and weeks later, still pondering a response. The questions help students think beyond their own identity, beyond the school community, and into how they fit into the world. These are questions that can be revisited throughout the year as middle schoolers experience new things, confront barriers, and bring new people into their "spark."

What Does This Mean for the Classroom?

A really important thing to remember and understand as an educator, especially in moments of frustration, is that the adolescent brain is not finished developing and is, in fact, in a period of significant growth. As Jay Giedd, an expert on adolescent brain development, said in a 2002 PBS *Frontline* documentary titled "Inside the Teenage Brain," educators shouldn't expect students to have adult-level skills in organization or decision making when their brain is still in the process of being built. This doesn't mean that you shouldn't have high expectations for students, but it does mean that they have to be taught and reminded about skills they are learning—both academic and social-emotional. According to Hermann Ebbinghaus's "forgetting curve," people tend to lose over half of what they learned in a matter of days or weeks and over 90 percent in one month unless they are actively reviewing the material (Woolliscroft, 2020, p. 251). This means that as educators we need to take time to explain the *why* behind what we are doing, share our thinking, and have students practice through taking on different roles, collaborating with their peers, and having "developmental experiences." According to the report *Foundations for Young Adult Success*, developmental experiences are opportunities for students to engage in learning that requires both action and reflection (Nagaoka et al., 2015). As students engage in these experiences, they make sense of what they are seeing or hearing, which then leads to their growth and development. Figure 1.1 shows the many ways that students can act and reflect in a classroom, including tinkering or contributing to take action, and connecting or integrating to reflect. As educators, we need to set the classroom conditions for developmental experiences and ask students to explain the stories they have constructed from their experiences so that we can understand the meaning they have made and how that might positively or negatively affect their future growth and outcomes.

FIGURE 1.1
Ways Students Can Act and Reflect in the Classroom

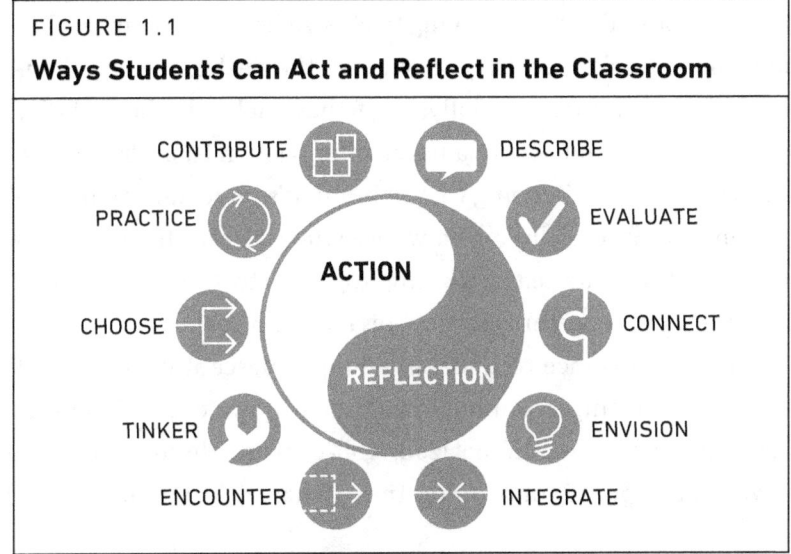

Source: From *Foundations for Young Adult Success: A Developmental Framework* (p. 39), by J. Nagaoka, C. A. Farrington, S. B. Ehrlich, & R. D. Heath, 2015, University of Chicago Consortium on Chicago School Research. Copyright 2015 by the University of Chicago Consortium on Chicago School Research. Reprinted with permission.

When I asked my former students what they remembered most about middle school, most mentioned either their friend group or an inspiring teacher who built a strong relationship with them. In thinking about those dynamics, another important thing to keep in mind is something that Camille Farrington, senior advisor at the University of Chicago Consortium, said in an interview (personal communication, November 15, 2023). She said that it's important not to pit students against their peers. Though this cautionary note may seem obvious, such divisions often happen in the classroom when a teacher labels a group of students as the "bad ones" (implicitly or explicitly). Farrington noted that peers have an outsized influence at this time in students' lives, and it is important to recognize the life they live outside the classroom. If students have to choose between being one of the "good kids" at the expense of being ostracized by their friends, ultimately having to choose between their teacher and their peer group, they may make the best choice academically but risk a cost socially; or if they make the best choice socially, that could lead to a negative impact on their grades and future outcomes. Keeping that in mind, it's important to build a community in the classroom where students see themselves as being on the same team, working together to support and help one another to master a concept or achieve a goal.

The importance of understanding adolescent development and incorporating that understanding into your classroom practice cannot be overemphasized. You can use the questions in Figure 1.2 to guide your exploration of this critical topic.

FIGURE 1.2

Finding the SPARK for Understanding and Using What You Learn About Adolescent Development

Study—Which topics related to adolescent development do you want to better understand? What questions do you have for your students after reading this chapter?

Pilot—What is one new thing you are thinking about doing differently in your classroom in response to the information in this chapter?

Analyze—What additional information do you need to help you better understand what your students are experiencing? Who can help you get that information?

Reflect—What are things you might be doing in your classroom that are either helping or harming students' development?

Kindle—What are new ideas you want to try in your classroom that may better meet the needs of students in this developmental time period?

2

Understanding Students' Thinking and Experiences: The Importance of Data

Data can be humanizing. Data can be liberatory.
Data can be healing.

—Shane Safir and Jamila Dugan, *Street Data*

It's a Wednesday at lunchtime. Six 7th grade students, who have been identified by their core academic teachers because they are struggling to turn in work, have been asked to talk about their experiences in school as part of a focus group. The room is a bright and cheery space, and the chairs are set up in a circle. The person leading the focus group is the school counselor, who these students have identified as one of their trusted adults in the building. The week before, the team had identified five core questions to ask in this focus group:

- What do you like most about our school?
- What do you like least about our school?

- When do you feel most confident in school?
- What is currently keeping you from being able to turn work in?
- What can your teachers do differently to help you be successful?

As students talked about their experiences, I sat off to the side of the circle taking notes to share with the team later. In their reflections, students said what they really liked was seeing their friends, and most mentioned liking at least one of the teachers in the building. They also mentioned how much they enjoyed their experiential education class and being able to work with their peers in all classes. Many talked about not liking the food in the cafeteria or how long they had to stand in line, and everyone found it hard to get from one side of the building to the other in a three-minute passing period. They talked about feeling confident when they knew the answer to a question or when it was a topic that really interested them.

When we got to the last two questions, though, students had even more detailed answers. In talking about what was currently keeping them from turning in work, one student mentioned that every teacher had a different policy for how work should be turned in during class and a completely different policy for how to turn in work if it is late. That same student mentioned that some teachers had a box in the back of the room to turn things in, others wanted it turned in online by 7 a.m. the day it was due, and still others walked around just checking for completion. And the late-work policies were even more confusing! He said some teachers didn't allow work to be turned in late at all, some took 50 percent off for late assignments, others allowed for work to come in until the end of the unit or quarter, and still others wanted a form filled out for every late assignment. He talked about how difficult it was to keep track of all those different policies. Other students in the circle jumped in to agree with him and shared that sometimes they didn't feel like they could even ask about the different policies because teachers would shut them down quickly, saying, "We went over this at the beginning of the year" or "It's in the syllabus." Students mentioned that the current situation made them feel stupid and like they would never get it right. As they reflected on what teachers could do differently, some mentioned having a uniform policy, across all teachers, regarding late work and turning in work. Others suggested reviewing the policy more often for the individual classes. Each of them said they wanted to do well but were having a hard time.

As I compiled the notes, I was amazed at how much we had learned in a 30-minute discussion and how valuable it was to ask the students these questions. As educators, we often assume so much about the motivations of our students without hearing directly from them. I was excited to share this information at the next team meeting and immediately started to think about how the counselor and I could present this information to our teammates in a way that wouldn't make them defensive and that could lead to some real changes to better support our students who were struggling with turning in assignments.

In this chapter, we will examine ways to gather valuable information from students to help inform next steps and how to use that information to co-create meaningful learning experiences and more positive environments for and with students. As you read the examples and reflect on your own classroom, keep in mind this important question: *How do I really know what my students are thinking?*

Attempting to truly understand students' thinking and their experiences in the classroom and the broader school environment can be both rewarding and frustrating for an educator. But working toward this understanding can make a huge difference and should come before any implementation of new strategies.

Levels of Data

The word *data* brings up various emotions for educators. Some love data and are ready to dig in and analyze responses because they have seen positive changes come from doing so or they just love numbers and making meaning from what at first seems to be a jumble of responses. Others may be more reticent because they have seen data used in punitive ways against educators and students or they don't understand what they are looking at in the mess of charts, graphs, and large spreadsheets. For these educators in particular, we need to take time to rebuild trust around data so that they understand what they are looking at and how it will be used. Researchers Dave Paunesku and Camille Farrington (2020) argue that "unfortunately, many teachers are accustomed to measures being used for punitive accountability purposes, which can make them hesitant to collect data that could reveal their own areas for improvement" (p. 17). What we need to remember as educators is that each piece of data collected often leads to more questions than answers, and it is only one small part of a larger story. If we collect meaningful data and use it effectively, then it truly can lead to positive changes for both students and educators.

During the COVID-19 pandemic and subsequent shutdown of school buildings, a lot of the traditional data that educators often used to make decisions was suddenly unavailable. Data such as that used for grades, attendance records, and standardized testing results were replaced by a more urgent need for understanding how students were feeling, finding out what families needed, or getting feedback on the best way to do remote learning. This period was understandably an extremely tough time for everyone, including teachers and students, but it did help to elevate the importance of qualitative data alongside quantitative data to truly understand the student experience.

In their book *Street Data: A Next-Generation Model for Equity, Pedagogy, and School Transformation*, authors Shane Safir and Jamila Dugan (2021) identify three levels of data. The first level is what they call "satellite data." As a teacher, I remember getting this type of data and never being sure how to use it effectively. It often consisted of scores for students I didn't have anymore, or the data sets were so large—on a district or schoolwide level—that they did not feel actionable for an individual classroom teacher. Though it is helpful to look at trends and overall areas of potential focus, this type of data on its own is often a lagging indicator and seems less helpful for a current class of students.

At the second level is what Safir and Dugan refer to as "map data." For me, this level of data was more actionable in my classroom, and it is often what you see educators using on a more regular basis. This type of data can be used to make decisions as an individual teacher or as a team to act on what students need in order to be successful. Because it is more focused, it can help teachers identify skill areas where additional instruction is needed or areas where students may need social-emotional support. This type of data often comes in the form of surveys or classroom-based assessments, along with current grades and attendance and behavior data, which can help teams and individual educators focus on more specific next steps. One thing that Paunesku and Farrington (2020) share about map data is the importance of educators making sure that they are using it in a way that is responsive to what students say so that students don't get "tired of expressing their opinions when it is clear to them that no one is listening" (p. 9). This often means sharing insights from the data with students, letting them know what changes are being made, or even asking additional questions when solutions or next steps aren't clear. Students have no idea how long their teachers spend in team meetings or as a staff poring over the data. Giving them explicit feedback or asking for clarification will help them to know someone is listening and will give them even more reason to share truthfully or put in more effort the next time they are asked.

The third level, and the one we are going to focus on most in this chapter, is what Safir and Dugan refer to as "street data." This type of data is more personalized and requires listening, observations, curiosity, and an open mind. Though it takes more time, this type of data collection allows teachers to hear from individuals and small groups of students to gain detailed, valuable insights like those gathered in the focus group highlighted in the opening of this chapter. As with map data, it is important for students to understand why you are gathering this information and how it will be used. Some of the most powerful changes to my classroom came from individual or small-group conversations with students during which they shared things that worked for them and things did not land the way I had hoped. From changing how I graded assignments to including more visuals and varying perspectives, my students made me a better teacher year after year. This type of improvement data allows for more immediate changes in teacher practice and is often more in a teacher's locus of control versus other forms of measurement data that often are communicated too late or in a way that is not digestible and actionable.

Data for Measurement Versus Data for Improvement

There are many ways to gather meaningful street data from students. In my work with the University of Chicago's Middle Grades Network, I have worked with teams of educators to use data effectively for change. From whole-class surveys, to smaller focus groups, to one-on-one empathy interviews, each of these methods can help educators better understand what students in their classroom are feeling, what will spark their learning, and what they find meaningful. It is important to keep in mind, however, that the data collected must be actionable for educators, and students need to believe that something will be done with what they've shared. Just because students have the opportunity to share their opinion doesn't necessarily mean that they feel heard. Improvement coach Curtis Taylor observed that it is important for the teacher to be vulnerable enough to say, "I want to improve my practice, and I need your help in doing that. And I trust you" (personal communication, November 30, 2023). We've all had the experience of taking a survey or participating in a focus group but then feeling like the resulting information went into a void because we never heard about the outcome or actions taken. This experience is frustrating for anyone, but especially for students, who often feel left in the dark or as though their voice doesn't matter.

In my interview with Sarah Gripshover, director of research at the Project for Education Research That Scales (PERTS), she noted that though collecting street data—measuring to improve—takes more time than more typical data collection, it can be a positive release from the norm. Teachers are "allowed to talk about it," and they don't feel trapped by the numbers related to data to improve (personal communication, October 30, 2023). They don't have to wonder why or hypothesize. Instead, they can be curious and ask questions to help make changes for the better.

Guarding Against Defensiveness and Feeling Safe with Data

Any time you collect data, especially from students, you will come across things that make you smile, things that make you think, things that make you sad, and things that involve every other emotion. In her book *Dare to Lead*, Brené Brown (2018) talks about the process of "armoring up" when you feel fear or that you are going to hear something that you do not want to. Here is how she explains the reaction:

> When we're in fear, or an emotion is driving self-protection, there's a fairly predictable pattern of how we assemble our armor, piece by piece:
>
> - I'm not enough.
> - If I'm honest with them about what's happening, they'll think less of me or maybe even use it against me.
> - No way am I going to be honest about this. No one else does it. Why do I have to put myself out there?
> - Yeah. Screw them. I don't see them being honest about what scares them. And they've got plenty of issues.
> - It's actually their issues and shortcomings that make me act this way. This is their fault, and they're trying to blame me.
> - In fact, now that I think about it, I'm actually better than them. (pp. 51–52)

To truly be able to analyze data and use it effectively, we as educators need to take off that armor and believe what students are saying. In working with teams, I often hear, "Well, the students must not have understood the question" or "Do they really know what that term means?" or "I think they were just clicking buttons and didn't take the survey seriously." And although each of those things may be true for some students, the majority are giving their honest opinion. Because of that, it's important not to dismiss the data you are getting and instead to think about how you can use it effectively in your classroom. Referring to a "mindset shift" for teachers, Gripshover said that it involves "giving students that expertise in their own perceptions and their own experience of school and not arguing with it" (personal communication, October 30, 2023). However, she added that the only way for teachers' engagement with this type of data to be effective is for them to feel safe and affirmed themselves. In other words, schools need to be open to having these types of conversations and supporting cycles of improvement and the effective use of qualitative data without weaponizing it.

Ways to Collect Qualitative Data

As previously stated, students want to share their voice. They want to feel like someone is truly listening to them. There are many ways to gather qualitative data, each with its own positives and challenges. So as you think about which will work best for you, keep in mind the following questions:

- What is my purpose in gathering this information?
- Am I in the right mindset to hear from my students?
- How much time do I have to gather the information I want?
- What support do I have to collect this information?
- How quickly can I analyze the data?
- What support do I have to analyze the data?

- How do I plan to share this information with students?
- What will I do with the information I gather?
- What support do I have to make the needed changes that students identify?
- And maybe, more important, am I in the right mindset to make changes to my classroom based on this information?

Student Reflections

In her math class, teacher Dora Medina uses a reflection tool every Friday to gather information from her students to better understand what they learned that week and how she can better support them in the following week. It's a simple chart that takes the typical K-W-L (Know, Want to Know, Learn) chart to the next level (see Figure 2.1). In her words, the chart gives her an opportunity to see if her students "enjoyed completing the activities throughout the week, or if they prefer partner work over independent work… and that helps me tweak my lesson for the next week.… It gives me an idea of what I could do differently" (personal communication, October 20, 2023). Medina said she especially uses the "How do I want to learn" question in the *L* part of the chart and shares with students how she has changed her approach based on their input, demonstrating how their voice is being used to shape instruction.

FIGURE 2.1
Reflection Version of a K-W-L Chart

K	W	L
What do I now **know** about this topic?	What do I **want** to know more about? What questions do I still have about this topic?	How do I want to **learn** this material?

This type of reflection can be done weekly, after an assessment, or even after a specific lesson. It can help teachers understand what was meaningful, what material stuck with students, and what may not have landed as intended. For all these types of data, though, the most important piece is bringing the information back to students and sharing what has changed due to their feedback.

To sum up, here are the positives, challenges, and things to keep in mind for student reflections as a form of qualitative data collection.

Positives

- Student reflections are meant to elicit short, quick feedback from students. Gathering this type of information can be done as a bellringer or as a closing activity in your classroom.
- This type of feedback can be gathered often and allows for immediate changes based on what you learn.
- Using the same questions every week enables you to see trends over time.

Challenges

- It takes time to review the information and plan for what to keep the same and what to do differently.
- Depending on the feedback you receive, you may have to shift your practice for just one class or for all your classes.
- You may get conflicting feedback from students.

Things to keep in mind

- Ask questions that will allow you to take meaningful action in response. If possible, ask the same or similar questions

each time you gather student reflections to see the trends over time.
- Try to keep this type of feedback/reflection to no more than three questions so that you have time to gather the relevant data points, analyze the information, and react to it promptly.

Student Surveys

Surveys are one of the most common ways to gather information from students. They usually consist of a series of different types of questions, including both open and closed responses. Most teachers have administered many surveys over their careers. Some surveys are mandated by the school, district, or state, whereas others are created by the teacher or a specific team in the building. Surveys are a way to gather information about the school as a whole, an individual classroom, a unit being studied, or the students themselves. Figures 2.2, 2.3, and 2.4 are examples of surveys that I used throughout my career.

Here are the positives, challenges, and things to keep in mind for student surveys as a form of qualitative data collection.

Positives

- Surveys are by far the fastest way to gather information from a large number of students. All students can take the survey at once, and you can often collect all the data during the same class period.
- You can ask more questions in a student survey than you typically can for any other method described in this chapter.
- The data collected can more easily be shared with students to gather their feedback, especially for closed-response questions, with charts or graphs for them to respond to.

FIGURE 2.2

Survey for the Beginning of the Year

Purpose: This survey gathers both vital and fun information about your new class of students. You can use the aggregate data from this survey to share commonalities or connections between your students, gather information about which units may be of particular interest, or think about additions you can make to your curriculum. For individual students, this survey helps you to understand their hopes, fears, and past experiences. Make sure you also give this survey to new students as they join your class throughout the year.

Sparking Connections and Understanding

All About You
- What name do you want to be called? Is this the same name you are called at home?
- How would your friends describe you in three words? Are those the same three words you would use to describe yourself? Why or why not?
- What's one thing you can do that you don't think anyone else in our class can do?
- If you had the opportunity to go anywhere for one day, where would you go? Who would you go with?
- When you think of a hero, who or what comes to mind? Why?
- If you could solve any problem in the world (big or small), what would it be? Why?
- What are you interested in doing in the future? (This could be a job, college, trade, or something else that you hope to accomplish.)
- If someone gave you $10,000, what would you do with it?
- What's your favorite color? How does that color make you feel?
- What's your favorite thing to watch? (This can be TV shows, movies, sports, YouTube, etc.)
- What do you like to listen to? (This could be music, podcasts, books.)
- What's the best thing you've ever read?

All About Your Home and Family
- Who do you live with? Family members? Pets? Anyone else?
- What responsibilities do you have at home?
- What other commitments do you have outside school (watching your siblings, sports, volunteering, chores)?
- What are your favorite things to do in your free time?
- Who do you go to if you need help or advice?

All About School
- What classes make you excited to come to school each day?
- What classes are hard for you to be excited about?
- What clubs and sports are you already involved in or interested in joining this year?
- If you could start any club or sport at our school, what would it be?

Understanding Students' Thinking and Experiences

- What would have to happen for you to feel like you've been successful this year?
- How do you learn best (reading, listening, seeing a visual, in groups, by yourself)?
- Finish this sentence: "If I could learn anything, I would like to learn more about _____."
- In past years, what is one thing your teachers did that you enjoyed or that helped you learn?
- In past years, what is one thing your teachers did that you did not enjoy or that made it harder to learn?
- What is your biggest hope for this year?
- What is one fear you have about this year?
- Is there anything else I should know?

FIGURE 2.3

Quarterly Survey

Purpose: You can use this survey to gather information each quarter to better understand how students are experiencing your class. Because it's administered quarterly, it gives you an opportunity to gather additional information from students when you might have more questions and to make changes if needed.

How's It Going So Far?

Please rate the following statements, with 1 meaning you strongly *disagree* with the statement and 4 meaning you strongly *agree* with the statement.

- I have learned a lot in this class this quarter. _____
- I have enough time to complete homework from this class. _____
- Tests and quizzes were connected to what we learned in class. _____
- The projects that were assigned were a good way to show my understanding of what we learned. _____
- I got the support I needed to be successful in this class. _____

Please share a little more about your experience in this class so far.

- What did you like most about this class this quarter?
- What did you dislike most about this class this quarter that I could change?
- What was the most meaningful assignment you did this quarter?
- What is one thing that you will take away from this class?
- What is one piece of advice you would give to students regarding this class?
- Is there anything else I should know?

FIGURE 2.4

Project Survey

Purpose: This type of survey is used to gather information after a larger project. You could create a similar one to use after finishing a unit or giving an assessment. The goal is to understand how students experienced that particular project (or unit) in order to adjust it for future students or to revise upcoming projects for your current students.

> **Project Survey**
> - What part of the project did you find most enjoyable? Why?
> - What part of the project did you find least enjoyable? Why?
> - (If applicable) On a scale of 1 to 4 (with 1 being *tough* and 4 being *amazing!*), how would you rate your group work? Why?
> - Where did you find yourself getting stuck? How did you get unstuck?
> - Do you feel you were successful in this project? How do you know?

Challenges

- Administering too many surveys can lead to students feeling overly surveyed, especially if they never see any impact or change based on their responses.
- Surveys generate a lot of data to analyze, which can be overwhelming.
- Oftentimes, survey analysis leads to more questions than answers.

Things to keep in mind

- Use a mix of closed- and open-response questions. Limit the number of open-response questions, as the responses are time-consuming to analyze.
- For closed, scaled responses, use a 1–4 rating scale with a description for each rating (e.g., 1, Strongly Disagree; 2, Disagree; 3, Agree; 4, Strongly Agree). Do not include a neutral response; eliminating that option requires

students to move toward one side of the scale, which leads to more useful data.
- Use questions that can be asked several times throughout the year. In their research on learning conditions, PERTS found that to use data to improve effectively, it takes at least three cycles of continuous improvement, including asking students for feedback, analyzing the data, and trying something new (Gripshover et al., 2022).
- Organize the survey by themes to make it easier to analyze.

Empathy Interviews

The goal of an empathy interview is to be able to truly hear what an individual student is saying through a one-on-one interaction. This practice uses a human-centered approach and should feel like an open conversation to gain a deeper understanding of a student's experience. These types of interviews should be structured around a specific learning goal you are trying to understand, but the questions should encourage storytelling and opportunities to dig deeper into the topic. Some examples of learning goals could be understanding how students who are newcomers are experiencing school or how a new grading policy is affecting students. If you have conducted a survey prior to selecting students for empathy interviews, you can also use information from the results to guide your goal selection. Figure 2.5 shows the typical arc of an empathy interview. These interviews typically take 25 to 30 minutes but can extend longer if the student has a lot to say.

As the figure illustrates, successful empathy interviews are structured around the following sequence of steps:

1. Introduce yourself to the student. Make sure to share some additional information about yourself if you don't

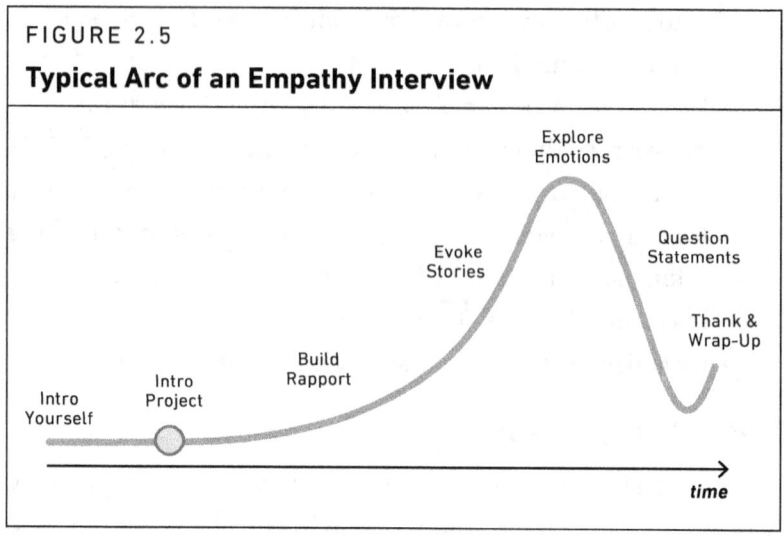

FIGURE 2.5
Typical Arc of an Empathy Interview

Source: From "Interview for Empathy," by M. Barry, n.d., Stanford d.School. Reprinted with permission.

already know the student or if you think it's helpful in setting the context for the interview.

2. Share the reason why you are conducting the interview. Explain as best you can what you are hoping to do with the information you are collecting.
3. Build rapport with the student. This step can be as simple as asking how their day is going or about an event that they participated in recently.
4. Have the student tell stories related to the topic you are hoping to learn more about. Remember, you are not trying to get a specific response but instead trying to gather information from their experiences and stories to better understand the area of focus. Use open-ended sentence starters such as these:

- Tell me about a time when you...
- What was a memorable (good or bad) experience you had when you...
- What might I find surprising or interesting about...

5. Explore the emotions that the student expressed while telling their story by asking what they were thinking about during a specific moment. This is often a time when the phrases "tell me more about" or "how were you feeling when" are useful, getting students to open up even more about their experiences.
6. Although empathy interviews are meant to evoke stories and not responses to a series of questions like a typical interview, at the end of the allotted time or when the student has finished sharing, you can ask follow-up questions or check for your own understanding. Just make sure that you are not supplying answers, influencing the conversation one way or another, or making the student feel like they said something wrong.
7. Thank the student and share any additional information about next steps.

Here are the positives, challenges, and things to keep in mind for empathy interviews as a form of qualitative data collection.

Positives

- This method allows you to hear from one student at a time and to select specific students that you may not often hear from.
- Answers to questions will often be more robust and detailed than those gathered in a focus group or survey.

Challenges

- Because you can engage with only one student at a time, empathy interviews take a lot of time, especially if you have a lot of students you want to speak to.
- You will not be able to interview every student and may miss some important voices.

Things to keep in mind

- When choosing students to interview, think about representing the diversity of your community and those whose perspectives are often left out.
- Be sure to include students who may have had very different experiences in your classroom or school. Doing so will help you to better understand the range of student perspectives and experiences.
- Use phrases such as "tell me more about" or "can you share additional experiences" to build on what the student has said.
- Avoid questions that imply a right or wrong answer.
- Embrace any silence in the interview. Allow enough time for the student to collect their thoughts or share additional information.
- Capture what you can during the interview without asking the student to repeat what they said. If the student feels comfortable having someone else taking notes, you can use that method.
- Give yourself time after the interview to debrief, especially if someone else was in the room. Together, fill in information that may not have been fully captured in the notes, or, if you were alone, quickly write down what you remember in order to expand and reflect on it later.

- Share themes and information related to your specific learning goal with other educators working on the same question.

Student Shadows

During a student shadow, an educator follows one student for an entire school day (when possible) in order to better understand the student's school experience through their unique lens. Like an empathy interview, this type of qualitative practice should also have a specific learning goal. In this case, you are trying to answer two questions:

- What is something you would like to learn about your school by shadowing a student?
- What type of student should you shadow to help you accomplish that goal?

Throughout the shadow day, the educator is both taking notes on the student's experiences and participating in the activities of the classroom with that learning goal in mind. Immediately following the shadow day, it is important for the educator to reflect on, analyze, and identify themes from the information gathered based on the learning goal. These themes and reflections should be shared with other educators to spark conversation and make changes to improve students' school experiences. Here are some questions that can be helpful to start the reflection and analysis:

- What did you observe?
- How often did the student interact with peers? Were those interactions positive or negative?
- How often did the student interact with their teacher(s)? Were those interactions positive or negative?

- How did the student show what they learned or understood during the day?
- What opportunities did the student have to reflect on what they learned throughout their day?
- How did this student's experience affirm your own idea about what happens in a school day?
- How did this student's experience challenge your own idea about what happens in a school day?
- How is what you experienced during the shadow activity the same as your own experience at that age?
- How is what you experienced during the shadow activity different from your own experience at that age?
- What might be the long-term impact on a student if they have days like the one you observed for the entire year or many years?

Here are the positives, challenges, and things to keep in mind for student shadows as a form of qualitative data collection.

Positives

- Student shadows can increase empathy for and understanding of students and what they are experiencing.
- The person shadowing can gather observations to generate insights and inform future initiatives and changes to improve students' experiences.

Challenges

- Clearing a whole day or even just a morning or an afternoon can be difficult for educators. It may require some creativity in covering classes in a specific grade level by an administrator, an instructional coach, or another staff member so that a teacher can be free to shadow a student

from another grade level. Schools can also use substitute teachers to cover a morning for one teacher and an afternoon for another so two teachers can have the experience of shadowing.
- Keeping an open mind can be hard, especially if a class period is not going well. Having a very specific learning goal will be helpful in staying in the moment.

Things to keep in mind

- Make sure that the teachers and staff whose classes you are visiting understand that shadowing is not an evaluation of them or their students.
- Inform the student you are shadowing about what you will be doing, and make sure they know that their participation is voluntary.
- Use an observation form that specifies your learning goal and any additional questions you want to keep in mind throughout the day. Take notes that include quotes and observations, but do not start to interpret or analyze during the shadow experience.
- Make sure you have the opportunity to reflect right after the observation and to share soon thereafter your learnings and wonderings with colleagues who are working on the same question that prompted your student shadows.

Focus Groups

A focus group is a guided discussion with a small group of students (usually five to eight has been the most successful in my experience) to gain a deeper understanding of a topic from their perspective. Focus groups are more structured than empathy interviews, and the goal is to understand why something is happening and how students think or feel about it in a detailed way. As with student shadows, a focus group should have a specified learning goal, but instead of being story based, focus groups should have a specific set of questions you want students' input on. As illustrated in the opening of this chapter, focus group questions should be based on other data you have collected (e.g., results from a survey, observations in your classroom, assessment results).

Here are the positives, challenges, and things to keep in mind for focus groups as a form of qualitative data collection.

Positives

- The questions are open-ended, which allows for more depth and nuance in the answers. Also, students can build from one another's ideas.
- Aside from hearing the answers to the questions, you can see nonverbal cues and group interaction, which gives even more context to what you are learning.

Challenges

- It can be hard to find a time when everyone you would like to include for a meaningful focus group is able to participate.
- Students are sometimes afraid to share what they really think about a class or the school because they fear it will be used against them.

Things to keep in mind

- Recruit students from different backgrounds and experiences who can provide unique perspectives about your learning goal.

- Make sure to get permission from each student and a member of their family. Share the purpose of the focus group and make sure students and families know they can opt out.
- Carefully consider who is facilitating the focus group and make sure they are trained to do so effectively. Trust is important in these conversations, and you want students to feel comfortable sharing their true thoughts and opinions. Ensuring this kind of environment may mean having a person, such as a counselor, who is trusted by students but not in the classroom every day facilitate the focus group.
- Have two notetakers in the focus group, if possible. Doing so allows for one to be focused on content, while the other is focused on body language and group dynamics.
- Start your focus group with an icebreaker to build rapport, especially if the students don't know one another.
- Ask open-ended questions. Questions that can be answered with a simple yes or no can stop the conversation prematurely and leave important points unaddressed. Open-ended questions allow participants to build on each other's thoughts and take the conversation in a new direction.
- Embrace the silence. Allow time for students to think of examples. Try not to fill the silence by sharing your own opinions or asking leading questions.
- Make sure that you follow up with next steps so that students understand that what they shared will help make the school better for everyone.

What to Do with the Collected Data

Once you have collected data, the next task is figuring out what to do with it. Here we consider some possibilities—one that involves educators working among themselves, and two that add students to the process.

Using a Protocol

One of the easiest and most effective ways to analyze qualitative and quantitative data is by using the "What? So What? Now What?" protocol. Introduced by educator Terry Borton in 1970 and further researched and developed by Rolfe and colleagues in 2001, this method has been used in many industries, including education, to foster curiosity and move systematically from noticing something to taking action. In the original protocol, which usually takes about 45 minutes to an hour to complete, analysis happens in three rounds:

1. Educators share only what they see in the data without judgment or analysis. The goal of this round is to stay objective and share concrete facts about what they are observing in their initial review of the data.
2. Educators share what they think the data mean.
3. In a move to action, educators identify potential next steps, additional questions, or changes that need to be made.

One helpful component that can be added before Round 1 is a brainstorm of inferences or questions that you are hoping to answer using the data. If you include this component, make sure to return to the inferences and questions at the end to see if what you predicted was correct or what you wanted to know more about was answered. The reason why this protocol is so effective is that by the end of the process, concrete actions have been identified based on evidence from the data collected.

Sharing Data with Students

One of the most effective practices that I have both witnessed and participated in as a teacher is sharing data with students in order to co-create a new practice for the classroom. These can include small changes, such as identifying multiple ways for students to comfortably share in class or identifying which learning platform they want to use to review for a quiz, as well as larger changes, such as revising the list of books read in the curriculum or modifying the schedule to accommodate more choice days during advisories. Whatever the purpose, students and educators can come together to create a greater sense of belonging, more opportunities for student voices to be heard, and better student–educator relationships.

Giving students the opportunity to analyze the data alongside their peers and their teacher can be challenging and exciting. It is important to have a tool that enables you to get the information you need and helps students to understand what they are looking at and how it relates to the data that were collected. Two tools that can serve these purposes are the 4, 2, Q protocol and data circles.

4, 2, Q protocol

As explained by improvement coach Curtis Taylor, the 4, 2, Q protocol has teachers sharing with students 4 celebrations drawn from the data, 2 areas of growth, and a question for improvement. As teachers share and students react, teachers hear the ideas for improvement directly from their students and also come to understand what students need from them. Taylor related that one teacher learned that her students thought she was "a little harsh" and needed "to be a little bit kinder and a little bit sweeter to us" (personal communication, November 30, 2023). Until she asked her students, this teacher had no idea that she was coming off that way. She responded by making some changes to her welcoming routines. As for the students in situations such as this, they felt trusted and heard. Taylor said that seeing their voices "being materialized in the classroom ... creates a partnership.... It keeps the teacher more accountable for their practice and moving away from deficit thinking" toward systems-level thinking (personal communication, November 30, 2023).

Data circle

Another strategy that I have seen used very effectively in my work in the Middle Grades Network is a classroom data circle. As with the 4, 2, Q protocol, the teacher pulls information from a larger data source to share with the class and gets feedback that leads to co-creating changes in the classroom. A typical data circle follows a specific sequence, as described here.

Setup. Join your students in forming a circle so that everyone is able to see one another. Identify a talking piece—a physical object that will be passed around the circle. Have the data that will be shared available in a form that is accessible to the students.

Opening the circle. Thank the students for being a part of the conversation and share the intent of the circle. In many of the schools that I've worked with, that intent is expressed with an opening statement like this: "You will have the opportunity to see the data and ask clarifying questions. I then want you to honestly share your thoughts, wonderings, and noticings. Finally, together we will identify next steps." During the opening, make sure to establish or review your community agreements, explain the talking piece and how to pass it around, and ask if the students need anything else to feel safe sharing their thoughts and opinions in the circle. Here are some examples of community agreements:

- Share: Share only your experiences, thoughts, and feelings.
- Listen: Listen to better understand your classmates.
- Patience: Everyone will get a chance to share. Make sure to respect the talking piece.
- Honor privacy: Ideas from the circle can be shared, but not individual names or stories.

Check-in question. Start with a check-in question to make sure everyone feels comfortable with the community agreements, process, and talking piece. This question can be something related to the data, or it can be more of an icebreaker, such as one of the following:

- Using a color, tell us how you are feeling today and why.
- What is the best book you've ever read or movie you've ever watched?
- How do you like to demonstrate what you've learned?

Questions about the data. Depending on the size of your class, you will probably have time for only two to four questions to cover in a class period. Choose questions to help shed light on things you want to understand more about from your students, based on the data that you collected. These can be areas of celebration or areas of growth. Show the students the specific data source and then ask the question to get feedback. Start with one student and then move around the circle, having the students pass the talking piece to one another. Once you make it around the circle, move to the next question. Be careful not to be judgmental about the data or students' responses; instead, express curiosity and let them know that you want their input to find ways to collaborate and make the class better for everyone.

Time for reflection. Many of the schools I've worked with have found it helpful to include an optional component at this point—an opportunity for students to write a reflection on their own or in pairs after the formal circle has concluded. The reflections provide you with a written record of students' thinking to help brainstorm next steps. The following prompts can be effective in helping students reflect:

- I notice... (What do you observe in the data?)
- I wonder... (What questions do you have about the data?)
- I think... (What do you think this means for our classroom or school?)

Closing with a purpose and next steps. Make sure to close the circle with an explanation of next steps, even if only to state that you are going to continue the conversation at a later date. You can also include a quote, a closing question, a share-out, or a positive affirmation if you have time.

After you share data with your students, whether through the 4, 2, Q protocol or data circles, make sure to return to it with specific action steps. Doing so may consist of taking their reflections and what you heard in the analysis to share changes you plan to make. It could also mean that you meet with a smaller group of students to generate ideas for changes and then have students vote on which one they want to see implemented. Whatever method you choose, make sure to come back after a few weeks or months to see how the changes you made have affected your students' experiences.

Things to keep in mind about sharing data with students

- **Be open and honest with yourself and your students.** Remember that whatever data you have collected is just one piece of a much larger story. Use processes like the "What, So What, Now What" protocol or data circles to continue to gather additional insights and iterate on next steps. Let your students know what you are working on and why you need their help in the process.
- **Start small and build.** You don't have to start with sharing data with your entire class or doing the entire 4, 2, Q protocol or data-circle process. You could start with a smaller group of students in order to practice and see what kind of feedback you get. You might also start with a 2, 1, Q, sharing 2 celebrations, 1 area of growth, and a single question; or just start with sharing the celebrations. In a modified data circle, you might start with just an opening, one round of data, and a closing. Sharing data with students can be an emotional experience as a teacher, so take your time building this into a sustainable practice.

Wrapping It Up

"Nothing about us without us" is a call to action with a long history that has spread from the disability community in the 1990s to the student-voice space today. The idea behind this slogan is that "no policies, from education reform, to employment protections, to better treatment and care in hospitals, should be created without the full and direct participation of those it affects" (Zarkhosh, 2024, para. 2). Numbers, graphs, and charts can give you information and may even help you start to plan, but the richness of qualitative data and research is what gives you the stories and a better understanding of the *why*. Qualitative data reminds you of the humanity behind the numbers and gives you the opportunity to ask questions and then co-create solutions alongside students, parents, and the community that is being affected. Take the time to ask questions, share, and truly listen; the effort is worth it. Use the questions in Figure 2.6 as a springboard to get started.

FIGURE 2.6
Finding the SPARK for Qualitative Data Collection

Study—How do you think these practices of gathering qualitative data would be received at your school? What opportunities and challenges do you anticipate based on your context?

Pilot—What is one method of data collection you could try in your classroom? What is something you want to understand more about your students? How might you share the data you collect with your students?

Analyze—How much time do you have to analyze data? Do you have anyone who can help you analyze the data?

Reflect—What are you worried about or excited about when it comes to the types of data collection and analysis methods shared in this chapter?

Kindle—How will you hold yourself accountable for the actions you decide to take?

3

The Power of Storytelling

> *Stories matter.... Stories have been used to dispossess and to malign, but stories can also be used to empower and to humanize. Stories can break the dignity of a people, but stories can also repair that broken dignity.*
>
> —Chimamanda Ngozi Adichie

It's the first day of school. Fifteen 7th graders are entering my classroom for advisory. As I stand at the door saying hello to them, I see a range of emotions. Some are excitedly talking, some look nervous, and still others look exhausted and not quite ready to end their summer. About a week before school started, I had sent them each a postcard introducing myself, welcoming them to our class, and asking them to bring a picture that represented something that was important to them. I told them it could be a person, a place, or a thing. It could be a real photo or something that they printed or found in another source, but to know they would be leaving it at school. I see a picture in most of their hands, but a couple of students quietly mention that they couldn't print theirs at home. I have them quickly send me the picture, and I print it for them so everyone has something that they can share.

As the bell rings, I explain that we are going to take some time to get to know one another using the pictures they brought. I tell them they can share as little or as much as they want about their picture and why whatever is featured is important to them. I start the sharing by taking out my own picture. It's a picture of the lake at our family's cabin in Wisconsin. I tell them that this is a place that means a lot to me because my grandpa bought the cabin for us to enjoy, and once he was gone, it was a place I could go and still feel close to him. I mention that it's the one place where I really feel like I can just get away and relax.

I then ask if anyone wants to go next. One brave student begins, and then the rest follow in quick succession. Over the next 30 minutes, students share about pets, vacations, family members, friends, sports teams, and their favorite places in Chicago. As more and more students speak, I can see that the quieter students are beginning to feel more comfortable. Students start to make connections to one another as they find out they have the same favorite baseball team or that visiting Michigan was something that they both had done that summer. We all post our pictures on the wall to begin to share our collective advisory story. In that moment, students begin to build connections through stories with me, their classmates, and the school community.

Stories Matter

From the passing of oral history from one generation to another, to visual stories in cave drawings, to early forms of writing in cuneiform or hieroglyphics, stories have always been a crucial part of what unites us and allows us to share our history, our culture, and our values in and beyond communities, across time, and throughout the world. As Rudine Bishop (1990) said in her article "Mirrors, Windows, and Sliding Glass Doors," stories give us mirrors to see ourselves, windows to see into the lives of others, and even sliding doors to walk through so we can experience aspects of another person's story. "Stories engage our thinking, emotions, and imagination all at once. As listeners we participate in the story with both mind and body as we enter the narrative world and react to it" (De Carolis et al., 2021, p. 472). Stories allow us to see one another's humanity, create connection, teach, and inspire. As Keisha Rembert (2023) shares in her book *The Antiracist English Language Arts Classroom*, the art of the story gives a shared knowledge and responsibility and often can "beget power, freedom, joy and resistance" (p. x). Stories can complicate a narrative so often written by the winners of history and tell a more complete and true story of our past and present. Stories make things "sticky" and memorable in a time when we are continually bombarded by information.

"Tell me a story" is something that every child says from the early stages of life. Made-up stories, stories about themselves, and stories about people they know often become a cornerstone of being able to make connections and learn about the world around them. As time goes on, the child becomes the storyteller and shares fantastical stories, stories about their day, and stories about what is happening to the people and places in their life with anyone who will listen. Educators of young students often use stories to introduce new concepts or reinforce what has been learned. But as students get older, story time is often replaced with more traditional academic activities, even though it may be just as important, or even more so, to use stories as students get older.

Scientists continue to learn more about what is happening in our brains when we hear and tell stories and to discover new facets of brain development in young adolescents. Stories mobilize different parts of the brain and cause hormones to be released, which is why storytelling is especially important and engaging for middle school students. As mentioned in Chapter 1, the adolescent brain is in a pruning stage during which certain synaptic connections are strengthened while others are lost, leading to a rewiring of the brain (Spear, 2013). Along with this continued plasticity and the rising levels of hormones, including dopamine, adolescents are at a prime time for new experiences, new perspectives, and new emotions. Dopamine can help regulate emotions and keep young adolescents engaged, while hearing stories causes the brain to release cortisol and oxycontin, which make the memories stick and create empathy (Peterson, 2017).

One challenge that many educators face is how to honor those individual stories, identities, and history that students bring to the classroom while also covering the mandated standards. This tension and emphasis on standards can lead to students feeling disconnected from what they are learning and teachers feeling disconnected from their students. This dilemma becomes even more true in middle school, when there are so many standards to cover and students are urgently trying to figure out their own story, who they are, and how they can contribute to the world around them in meaningful ways. Middle schoolers live in constant tension between childhood and adulthood. Young adolescents are starting to pull away from their families but still need their love and support. They are working to establish healthy relationships with their peers while struggling to make and maintain those friendships. And they are beginning to think about what the future holds while often being overwhelmed by all the choices and mixed messages they are receiving in and outside school.

Honoring Our Students' Stories

In this time of figuring out who they are, middle schoolers want to see themselves reflected in what they are learning. They want to know that their individual story matters. Like all of us, middle school students want to feel seen, heard, and valued. Oftentimes nobody's asking students in the school context about their lives in any amount of depth. "And so that becomes really, really important to them. That somebody is seeing them and actually asking them what's going on inside" (Jenny Nagaoka, personal communication, October 10, 2023). There are many ways, big and small, to bring out those stories in the classroom and to build community, value students' experiences, and enhance the curriculum.

Building a Collective Story

"Sharing our stories is the ultimate act of community building, respect, and shared humanity" (Rembert, 2023, p. 39). As described in the opening of this chapter, to build a collective story from the first day of a school year, I had students bring in a picture of someone, something, or a place that was important to them. We shared those pictures and the stories behind them before making them into a collage on the classroom wall. It was the first decoration that went up for the school year, and the activity gave ownership of our classroom to the students and their voices and honored them as people. As the year progressed, students would refer back to those stories and share new ones that connected to their original pictures and to the stories their peers shared. We would add new pictures to the wall at different times to continue to build our collective story.

Taking a Pulse Check

A quick way to give students a daily opportunity for storytelling is to do a pulse check in the form of a share-out at the beginning of class. This can consist of displaying different memes or emojis for students to identify with and then share why they are feeling that way using questions such as these:

- Which of these pictures most closely represents how you are feeling today? What is making you feel that way?
- What story can you tell from your day that relates to one of these pictures?
- If you were to describe your feelings about what we are learning using one of these pictures, which one would you choose and why?

Each of these gives students a chance to share something about themselves and for you as an educator to gather information on how students are feeling that day in order to inform instruction.

Asking a Question of the Day

Another opportunity for daily storytelling is to have a Question of the Day that allows students to write or talk about themselves in meaningful ways. Their responses can be shared through journal writing, in pairs, in small groups, or in community-building circles. Including such activities as part of the daily lesson elevates students' voices and honors their lived experiences.

Many educators have creative ways that they use storytelling in their classroom. Cathy Gormley likes "to do either storytelling or story sharing to help students learn how to build empathy and listen to other people, because even in 8th grade we know that they really struggle with that" (personal communication,

November 6, 2023). Another educator, Naomi Wilfred, starts the year with a choice of prompts, including "You've got to try this…" or "Who's your most important person in the world," giving students the opportunity to share something that is really significant to them or that they are really good at doing (personal communication, December 8, 2023). Here are some other ideas for daily prompts that elicit stories:

- What is an experience you have had that included food as an important part of the story?
- Think of a time when you were exploring your city, town, or neighborhood. What did you find that was memorable?
- When is the time that you felt the most celebrated?
- What experience have you had that enabled you to give back or volunteer?
- When have you connected to something that you have learned in school?

These types of questions lead to opportunities for students to connect to one another and for educators to learn more about their students and what motivates them.

Things to Keep in Mind

- **Keep it quick and frequent.** Time always seems to be in limited supply in schools. Storytelling does not need to take up a lot of time, and it adds a lot of value as the classroom community learns more about its members. Things like taking a pulse check and asking a Question of the Day can take less than 10 minutes and may be done at either the beginning or end of class.
- **Use the information gained from storytelling in your lessons.** As you learn your students' stories, use the

information to make connections in class. If you find that your students are interested in healthcare, make sure to include information about what healthcare was like in the time periods you are studying, or use statistics from the healthcare field in your math or science class. If they talk about their hobbies outside school, find relevant articles or books to include in your classroom library. It's amazing what you can learn and how valued students feel when they know their stories have been heard.

Sharing a Bit About Yourself

Often you hear about the funny moment when a young student realizes that their teacher doesn't live at the school and actually goes grocery shopping or to the movies just like the student does! Or that shocking moment when a student runs into their teacher at an event or walking down the street with their dog. Students want to know that their teacher is a real person who has triumphs and makes mistakes. They want to know what their teacher is passionate about in the curriculum and how it connects to their life.

As a history teacher, often after a trip or a weekend excursion, I would come back with information about some historical site that I visited or something new that I had learned. My students were always interested to see the slideshow or artifacts that I shared with them and to understand the background story, which often made an abstract concept more concrete. For example, when we were studying immigration, I talked about my great-grandparents and their trip from Norway, and how they struggled with the language and the culture after arriving in the United States. During our study of the Holocaust, I shared pictures from my visit to Dachau. I talked about how distressing it felt to be in that camp and see the houses and neighborhood surrounding the barren land where barracks used to stand, knowing the number of people who were imprisoned and killed there. And in our study of the fighting in World War II, I would share my grandpa's experience as a Marine in the Pacific Theater and the biases he developed against people of Japanese ancestry. We talked about how he worked to overcome those biases over many years following his return from Japan and how long it took for him to share his war experiences with others. As a class, we would talk about what it means to learn from history and how individual stories can help humanize historical events.

In my classroom there were pictures of my family and drawings and art created by my children. I added my own pictures and stories to our wall at the beginning of and throughout the year. I shared books that I was reading, places where I was volunteering, and other events that were relevant to what we were studying. My students definitely did not know, or need to know, everything about my life, but they certainly had a window into things we had in common or that I was passionate about. This knowledge led to stronger teacher–student connections, which in turn led to them opening up and sharing when they had a connection to what we were learning or even when they were struggling with something in or outside class.

Things to Keep in Mind

- **Test the waters.** The goal of sharing a bit about yourself is for your students to know that you are a real person and have interests, thoughts, and ideas similar to theirs. If you are uncomfortable with the thought of sharing information about yourself, test the waters by starting with small things, such as where you went to college, your favorite sports team, what you are reading, or your favorite food. This gives students a point of connection without you having to reveal too much about yourself.

- **Connect to the curriculum.** As mentioned, much of what I shared in class was connected to the curriculum. Your stories, like your students' stories, help the curriculum to come alive. A brief anecdote during a history lesson about a place you visited, or something you saw in nature that you mention during a study of botany, or a book you read on a topic will help solidify a connection that students can hang their knowledge on.
- **Know your boundaries.** Building authentic, developmentally appropriate relationships with students is important, but so is maintaining a productive environment for learning. Understanding what boundaries you need to maintain to have effective classroom management is key. This boundary looks different for every teacher. For me it meant sharing the pieces of my story that were connected to what we were learning and listening when students had something to share. This approach helped me to build connections to my students and to the content, while also making sure that they understood that I wasn't their friend and that there were expectations for what we were going to accomplish in class. Maintaining the delicate balance between bringing joy and your lived experience to the classroom and maintaining the structures you need to foster learning is something that takes time and experience to learn and develop.

Storytelling Throughout the Curriculum

Narrative writing is often thought of as the best way to bring storytelling into the classroom. Students brainstorm stories from their past and then write about them in a compelling way. They peer edit, get feedback, and sometimes share them aloud. And though this is an effective approach, there are many other ways to bring storytelling into the curriculum across all content areas.

In literature, students can explore characters who are struggling and celebrating in similar and different ways compared with their experiences. Dialogue journaling is an effective way to give students an opportunity to tell their stories and explore connections to what they are reading. In a dialogue journal, a teacher gives the student a piece of writing to respond to through a free-form journal response or with a prompt. The teacher then responds to the student with questions, comments, and additional connections. The conversation continues through writing back and forth, allowing for individual connections to be made between teacher and students and for new stories to be told.

In social studies, I would often use a children's book to introduce topics and historical time periods to my class. It turns out that students love to be read to at any age, and children's books often give enough context to help all students start with the same base-level background knowledge needed to jump into a new topic. Books can open doors to different types of people, cultures, ideas, and perspectives or help affirm the identities of the students in the room.

Another option for creating a shared sense of background knowledge is to start each time period or unit with students asking a family member two or three questions about the designated topic and bringing the responses back to share in small groups or in a whole-group class discussion. For a fairly recent event, those questions could be about what the family member remembers or how they felt about the event. For more distant events, family members could share connections they have, what they know about the event, or even how it connects to things still happening today. If possible, you could also identify expert family members, staff members, or community members and invite them to come in and discuss topics that you are studying. The person could be someone who works in a field connected to the event or topic or someone who lived through a specific time period or event.

In science or math, storytelling can be used to introduce a difficult or complex subject. Students are often looking for ways that they can use what they are learning in school in their everyday life. Stories about scientists and mathematicians who look like them and are trying to solve problems like those they are working on can help build those connections, making the concepts come alive in a way that the textbook cannot. A story about how a math concept can be used in real life can also help students see the relevancy of a topic. And learning the story of how a scientist or mathematician got into their job can even help open up new career possibilities for students.

To build relevancy in all subject areas, teachers can use storytelling on a weekly basis to have students share ways that they have used what they have learned in class in their daily lives. Through activities such as turn-and-talks, exit slips, or whole-group discussions, students can share stories of how they are connecting to what they are learning and where they have seen more abstract concepts show up in their lived reality.

Things to Keep in Mind

- **You don't need to change your entire curriculum.** Implementing storytelling doesn't mean that you must change your entire curriculum; instead, it means adding parts that help humanize the topic you are studying. Taking a few minutes to read a children's book, share a story about how a concept can be used in real life, or let students share their own connections makes the topic more relevant to students.
- **Students bring their own stories to your curriculum every day.** Whether you build in storytelling or not, students are building their own narrative every day in your classroom. Sometimes the narrative is that what they are learning is boring or not related to their lives outside school. Sometimes the narrative is that they know exactly where they will use this concept or idea in their life and can't wait to share what they are learning. Providing opportunities to share both of these narratives will help some students to find relevancy, while others will build even greater connections to what they already know to be meaningful.

Bringing in Stories from the Community

Another powerful set of stories often exists right outside the classroom door. Opening learning beyond the room's four walls can give students a new perspective on their community and their world, while forging new connections and creating opportunities for empathy and understanding.

The community where I taught was home to the Illinois Holocaust Museum and Education Center. That proximity allowed us to both visit the museum and invite Holocaust survivors to share their stories with our students. One of these memorable visits was from Aaron Elster, a survivor who later passed away in 2018. As he shared his story of being hidden in an attic throughout the war, students were both saddened and angry that he had had to endure these conditions. They asked him what he wanted to tell students like them. He told them to be nice to others and to be aware that you can make a difference. As he said, "We are always in a moment when we can take action; the question is, will we?" This message stuck with me and with my students long after he walked out of the gym that day.

Another opportunity for storytelling came from an interim principal in my building. In a meeting, we were discussing my curriculum for the spring, and he shared that he and his family had escaped from East Germany after World War II. He said that during the war his dad had been a prisoner of war in Siberia, while his mom spent the war living in a German town. He said that after they made it to the United States, his parents both became very active in the civil rights movement. Given the complexities and connections that were evident in his story, I asked if he would be willing to share it with my classes, and he readily agreed. He came to all five of my classes and shared his story, even taking tough questions about his dad serving in the German military, his mom living in a town near a concentration camp, and what it was like to escape from Communist rule as a young child. This story gave students a different perspective and complicated the simpler narrative they had constructed.

Sometimes the best visitors are members of your own family. Educator Naomi Wilfred said her mother would come to her classroom and "tell her stories of opening her school. She told stories about her trips to Africa. And then she'd do an 'I am' poem with them.... We used to always do the poem, 'I'm a great somebody,' [by Adrienne Sealy Hardesty] and then she... did it with my students when I was teaching them. That was... such a beautiful full-circle moment" (personal communication, December 8, 2023).

Leaders from local nonprofit organizations, government officials including a congresswoman and a mayor, as well as songwriters and a variety of authors came to speak to my students. Hearing from people outside the school helped the curriculum come alive and allowed students to imagine different possibilities for what their futures could be in the stories that were shared.

Things to Keep in Mind

- **Find storytellers in your community.** Not every community has access to a museum dedicated to what students are learning about, but every community does have local people with a story to share. Whether it's the person who started a nonprofit to build mini-libraries or deliver baked goods to people in need or a veteran who served in the military or a person who wants to share more about their heritage, their stories are important catalysts for engaging students in learning.
- **Ask your colleagues and students for ideas for speakers.** You don't have to find potential visitors on your own. If you want to have more outside voices in your classroom, ask people for ideas. You could ask students to identify an interesting local person they would like to hear from, or get ideas from something that a student shared in class or from a lunchtime conversation with your colleagues. Use your resources to assemble a "speakers' bureau" that you can reach out to year after year.

- **Understand the protocol for bringing in visitors.** Every district has a different protocol for visitors. Give yourself plenty of time to contact the person you want to invite, get any information that administration needs in order to bring the person in, and confirm all the details with your visitor. You can bring in visitors virtually, which can be easier for scheduling but still may require permission from administration and families.
- **Prep visitors before they come to speak with your students.** Making sure that the person understands a little about your class, what background knowledge students have, and what kinds of questions they may ask is very important in setting up a successful classroom visit. Also make sure that visitors know how much time they have to share their story and what type of engagement they will have with students. Here are a few logistics to think about and share:
  — Who will be facilitating the visit?
  — Where should the visitor go upon arrival?
  — Will the visitor be speaking at an all-school assembly, or will they only see one group of students?
  — Will there be a designated Q&A, or will you have already collected questions from students to ask that you can share before the visit?
- **Prep your students for the visit.** Make sure students understand who the speaker is and why the person is coming. Give them an opportunity to formulate questions and clear up any misconceptions. Make sure to talk through audience participation and the expectations for after the visit (will they write thank-you notes, share a reflection, or use this information in an upcoming assignment).

The Power of Students Sharing Their Family History

Many of the people I spoke with as I started writing this book talked about a memorable project from middle school being one in which they got to share their family's heritage or a story about their family with their classmates in a meaningful way that connected to the curriculum. For example, my cousin said that her most memorable project was one in which she shared her heritage through posters, cultural dress, and food. Our grandpa even came for the event!

Feeling like you belong and that your family is welcomed and respected in the school community is one of the most important components of academic and nonacademic success. In the report *Foundations for Young Adult Success*, the researchers reiterated this idea through their findings that students who believe they are recognized and valued members of their academic community will better engage in their learning. That strong sense of belonging has also been connected to continued success in school, whereas students feeling unwelcome or threatened has been linked to poorer performance (Nagaoka et al., 2015). Creating positive learning conditions and building a classroom culture of inclusion allows students to experience that feeling of belonging.

One of the most effective ways that I found to honor my students' stories and their unique identities—while still fostering that sense of belonging—was through a family history storytelling project that was integrated into our study of immigration, migration, and major events throughout history. In this project, students were given a set of questions to use to interview a family member of their choice and then had options for how to share their family's story with our school community. They could focus on a family member who had immigrated to the United States or center their project on a family member who had lived through a major event in history. This assignment gave students an opportunity to see the historical events not just as words on a page but as real people experiencing the trials, tribulations, and triumphs of life.

For those who were interviewing a family member who immigrated, the questions they asked included the following:

- What country are you originally from? What was life like for you there?
- What early experiences stand out for you from your childhood?
- What is one major event that happened in your country that you remember from before you left?
- Why did you leave?
- When did you leave? How old were you at that time?
- How did you prepare to come to a new country?
- What changes in lifestyle did you make when you came here?
- What customs have you kept?
- What do you miss from your homeland?
- What was your first impression of the United States? Has this initial impression changed over time? Has it changed for the better or for the worse?
- If you had to give one piece of advice to someone immigrating to the United States today, what would it be and why?

For those interviewing a family member about a time period or event, the questions included the following:

- Describe the event. When did this occur? Where were you? What happened?
- Who were the influential people during this event? What types of things did they do to either help or hurt the United States? What did they do to help or hurt the world?
- What was the immediate impact of the event (on the day it happened) on your own life?
- How did the event change your life over the long term?
- How did the event change what was happening in the United States or the world?
- Where did you live when this event happened (city, state, type of home)?
- Who lived with you during this event?
- What was your daily life like during this time period? Did you work? Were you in school? What was your daily routine?
- What did people do for fun during this time? What types of entertainment were common (with friends, with family)?
- How did the event affect what you were able to do and not do?
- Who was your best friend at this time? How did that person fit into your life/this event?

These questions served as a guideline for the interviews, and students could add or skip questions depending on who they were talking to. These questions were meant to help students not only better understand the events but really understand the humanity of the people who were living through them. Many of my students were hearing these stories for the first time and had no idea that their family members experienced what they did.

Students also had a choice in how to share their learning with our school community. Their options included the following:

- A scrapbook in which students shared photos of their family and told their story through those photos.
- A children's book in which students illustrated their family story.
- A memory box in which students shared items that illustrated key parts of their family's story and how those items connected to what was happening in the world at that time.
- A short movie that included photos, items, interviews, or other ways to share the story they were trying to convey.
- A podcast that included background history, the family story, and how those events affected their life then and today.
- Letters back and forth between two family members that the student created to show two different perspectives and experiences from their family's story.
- Diary entries in which the student took one perspective and showed how their family member was experiencing the events.

Once students completed their interview and chose their project, they then wrote a narrative in the voice of their interviewee. Earlier in the year students had written a fictional narrative, so they understood the narrative arc and the components of a story. Students started by determining the conflict their interviewee faced and then identified the climax. From there, they identified the *who, what, when, where, why,* and *how* before beginning to write. Using the information they had received from their family member, students were able to include rich details and even direct quotes from the person. They then used this narrative as the script for putting together the project they chose.

After completing their projects, students presented their stories in a variety of ways. During one week, we took time in class for each student to share their family story and gather "celebrations" and questions from their peers. Each student was given a "glow book" at the end of their presentation that compiled those celebrations. The week of project presentations was always one of my favorite weeks of the year, as students' faces lit up as they shared their stories, personal items, experiences, and connections to the history we had been learning about in class. Other opportunities for sharing included project displays throughout the school and in the library, presentations of projects to elementary school students in the district, and postings of projects on an internal website where families could see all the stories in one place. Each of these opportunities brought our community together and broke down barriers as students and families saw the similarities in their stories.

At the end of this project, students reflected on what they had learned and how it affected them. Often these reflections were even more enlightening than the project itself. Sometimes the reflections showed a better understanding of their parents. One of my former students described it this way:

> I have learned from my mom's story that sometimes it is hard to make a decision we don't want to make, but we have to suck it up and just do it. So now I view my mom in a different light. I view her now as a selfless individual. So Mom, I don't know if you'll ever read or see this, but thanks for making the decision of marrying Dad and having my siblings and me.

Sometimes students better understand not only their family members but also the history that was happening around them.

In this reflection on Japanese internment camps in World War II, another former student shared the following:

> Doing this immigration project was a really good experience for me. I learned a lot about my family's past that I never knew before. When I first got the project, I thought it would be no fun and very boring, but then I learned some really important information and I thought about what my grandpa and his family really had to go through. He was only a little older than me and was put into a jail when he was innocent.... This project has really changed my life and has taught me many things that are rarely written in school textbooks.

One of the most memorable reflections came in the second year I facilitated this project, when a student wrote the following reaction to hearing about his dad's journey from Cambodia during the Khmer Rouge regime:

> After learning all of this information, I have a lot more respect for everyone in my family, the Cambodian people, and their struggles in order to survive in Cambodia. I have come to appreciate my parents more and all that they have done in order to provide me with the life that I have today.... From what I have learned, I finally realize why my dad cannot find the strength to return to the country that had taken his parents and childhood away from him, as well as many other Cambodian people.

That student came back years later to see if I still had his project and reflection. What he had learned had affected him so much that he had found a volunteer position at a museum dedicated to Cambodia and wanted to use the project to help share his story. He hoped to help others understand the hard history that so many in that country had faced and to be part of an institution that celebrated his family's culture.

Another student said her project helped her understand women's suffrage and the fight for equal rights more than what she had learned in the textbook. In the last few lines of her reflection, she said, "This project changed my outlook, and it's made me more appreciative of my family. It made me think. And isn't that the REAL criteria for a good project?"

Things to Keep in Mind

- **Students may feel they have no one to interview.** Sometimes one of my students would say that they didn't have someone to interview, perhaps because they thought their family was "boring" or their family member wouldn't want to answer the questions. Usually I could address the challenge with a call to the student's home or by brainstorming with the student about a time period they were interested in learning more about. Every so often, though, the student really didn't have anyone to interview. In a situation such as this, it's important to have some teachers or community members who are ready to offer their story to students. We were lucky enough to have long-time teachers who were willing to share about how the school had changed over time, or how they or their students had reacted to a historical event, or even their own family's journey to the United States. It was always fun when students shared a story about someone in the building, as it created a bond between students and educators and honored the stories that existed within the school community.
- **Communicate early and often with students' families about this type of project.** I mentioned this project at events early in the school year, such as open house, and then sent home a letter, in both digital and printed form,

when I introduced the project to my classes. It is important to let families know that students will be bringing home a list of questions to ask a family member and what will be expected of the student following the interview. If the project options will include students bringing in objects from home, also be sure to let families know where those objects will be stored and when they will get them back, especially if they are being displayed. The more information you can provide, the more successful this type of project will be. Figure 3.1 is an example of a letter to families.

FIGURE 3.1
Sample Letter for Family History Project

Dear 7th grade families,

Today in class your student received their family history project assignment. This is always an exciting time of year where we get to learn more about one another and the people who make up our community through the tradition of oral history. Oral histories are created when one person interviews another person about a specific time period in the interviewee's life or a specific topic they can recall. The interviewer then takes the interviewee's responses and creates a text (in this case a narrative) told from their point of view, capturing both their voice and spirit.

Much of what we study in history is what is considered "traditional" history, or the history of major political figures, important historical events, and significant historical trends. In this project, our school community will help tell the history of the everyday people who make up our world and how they were affected by a specific event or time in their life. For the next month, your student will be working on finding out a little more about your family history and turning those new understandings into a narrative project to share.

Students will be using the attached questions to interview a family member and make a choice about which project to complete. Please read through this information with your student to make sure that the project chosen is one that makes sense, given the person being interviewed. If you have concerns about this project, please reach out to me at [email address] or [phone number].

I hope this leads to a great discussion where many stories are shared.

With gratitude,

[Teacher name]

- **Share the timeline for when each part of the project will be due, from the interview to storyboards to the final project.** A timeline will give you ample time to check in with students and see where they are struggling long before the final project is due. Here is an example of due dates that I gave my students:
  - 10/22—Project introduced to students and families
  - 10/24—Project option selected
  - 10/30—Interview questions due
  - 11/5—Storyboard/narrative plan due
  - 11/12—Narrative due
  - 11/15—All photographs/pictures/images due
  - 11/18—Draft personal reflection due
  - 11/18–11/22—In-class work days
  - 11/25—**Project due,** including final personal reflection
  - 11/25—In-class presentations begin
- **Give students checklists and rubrics to help make sure they are on track and can assess their own project and learning.** Here is an example of a checklist that I used for my students:
  - Does your title slide, page, or opening include your name, who you interviewed, and a creative title for your project?
  - Does your project take us through a narrative that includes direct quotes from your interviewee, an exposition, a conflict, the rising action, a climax, the falling action, and a resolution?
  - Does your project include a personal reflection with what you learned in doing this project about your family, the time period, and yourself?

— Does your project include pictures and other thoughtful items connected to your family or the time period you were asking them about?
— Have you checked your spelling and grammar before turning in your project?
— Have you saved your project using the correct format and in the correct spot?

When assessing these projects, I used individual rubrics for each project type. The rubric had a five-point scale ("exemplary" to "missing") and included categories related to the following:
— The narrative arc and effective use of storytelling using the interview responses
— Photographs and/or pictures to help illustrate the story
— The personal reflection
— Speaking, expression, and volume
— Grammar and spelling

- **Some students may feel uncomfortable sharing their story.** Being vulnerable to classmates, even ones your students have gone to school with for many years, can be difficult. If you assign a project like this one, make sure it is not the first time your students have had to share something about themselves in your class. Model that sharing with them and give them multiple opportunities to connect whatever they are learning to themselves and to share those reflections with others throughout the year. If students were really reluctant to share, I would give them the opportunity to record themselves and then play the recording in class. And on rare occasions, especially for students who had accommodations or needed significant extra support, I would have them choose a smaller group of students to share their story with instead of sharing in front of the entire class.

- **Help students learn how to give appropriate feedback.** One powerful part of being the storyteller is receiving the questions, feedback, and celebrations from peers. Giving this type of feedback can be difficult, as students often don't know what to say. Sometimes the comments are generic—for example, "Good job" or "I liked your pictures." And sometimes the feedback is too specific or too personal. To address these shortcomings, give students sentence starters and ideas for what type of feedback to give. Here are some starters that helped my students to home in on a particular aspect of their peer's project:
  — I really liked how you...
  — It was really interesting how you...
  — I wonder more about...
  — I noticed that you...
  — It was clear that you worked hard on...
  — One question I still have is...

  Before having students share their stories, it's also important to have a conversation about what type of feedback they would want to get in order to help them craft helpful insights to share with their peers. I did this by having students answer the following three questions during a think, pair, share class discussion and then recording the themes on chart paper for students to refer back to during the presentations:
  — When have you found feedback to be most helpful?
  — What makes feedback helpful?
  — What makes feedback unhelpful?

It's important to have students give feedback to one another throughout the year to build this muscle.

Wrapping It Up

Revisiting the powerful words of Rudine Bishop (1990), books and stories may not solve all the world's problems, but they can "help us to understand each other better by helping to change our attitudes towards difference" (p. xi). Stories and storytelling unite us as humans and are a powerful way to create a sense of belonging and community, which can help students find meaning in what they are learning each day at school. Use the questions in Figure 3.2 to get started on using the power of storytelling to spark student interest.

FIGURE 3.2
Finding the SPARK for Using Storytelling in the Classroom

Study—What stories could help make your curriculum come alive for students? Do you have people in your community who could help tell those stories?

Pilot—How can you bring your students' identities and stories into the classroom? What are relevant stories that you can share about your own life?

Analyze—What data, both qualitative and quantitative, can you collect to help you understand the impact on your classroom community of students sharing their stories?

Reflect—How did it feel to use storytelling in your classroom? For you? For students?

Kindle—What are other ways you can bring the concept of storytelling into your classroom or into your school community?

4

Integrating the Arts

Art can help us understand our history, our culture, our lives, and the experience of others in a manner that cannot be achieved through other means. It can also be a source of inspiration, reflection, and joy.

—National Museum of African American History and Culture,
The Importance of Visual Art

It's a Thursday afternoon during what has been a particularly tough week. Students have been disengaged during class and don't seem to be understanding the legacy of the Harlem Renaissance in the way I had hoped; they aren't seeing why it was such a pivotal golden age for Black artists, musicians, and writers. All week long I have been trying to explain how important this time period was in elevating Black voices and experiences for the first time in U.S. history. As I reflected on my own teaching and looked through exit slips, I realized that I had spent too much time lecturing and having students read about these individuals, but not enough time letting students actually hear from the artists themselves and experience the powerful music, artwork, and writing that influences so much of our society today.

I immediately decided to scrap my plans for Friday and began pulling together resources to make my new plan come to life.

As my students walked into class on Friday morning, they were surrounded by the music of the Harlem Renaissance, with art and poetry hanging on the walls. We spent the entire class period experiencing the products of the Harlem Renaissance instead of just reading about them. The students listened to the artists describe their own experiences. They reacted to what they heard, made found poetry from longer pieces, and spent time analyzing how the art created during the Harlem Renaissance told the story of everyday people and elevated their experiences. Watching them react to what they saw and heard, I also witnessed the "aha" moment of understanding as to why this time period was an important awakening in our cultural history and how it continues to influence what they see and listen to today.

Why Art?

Middle schoolers are often engaging with many forms of art, including listening to music, watching or creating a video, designing a digital world, or looking at and editing images. From the newest meme to the most recent trends, art is an ever-present part of their lives every single day. They use it to communicate, to process, to decompress, and to be entertained. Therefore, using art in the classroom can be a powerful tool for increasing student engagement while bolstering a sense of belonging and giving students developmental experiences that allow them to try new things, practice new skills, and reflect on next steps.

Arts education is an area that offers more freedom to explore a lot of different types of things in many different ways. As Jenny Nagaoka, the deputy director of the UChicago Consortium on

School Research, explained, students are more willing to take risks and see art as a safe space to explore their identity or new ideas that they aren't necessarily comfortable with yet (personal communication, October 11, 2023). Many students and teachers see an almost magical aspect to arts-based thinking, which can lead to even more powerful learning in a classroom.

When asked why art can be such a powerful teaching tool, an art teacher explained that students are often looking for people who want to hear their idea and to recognize that their creativity and their ideas have weight (Meredith Kachel, personal communication, November 20, 2023). Opening that world and integrating arts-based thinking into your classroom gives students the freedom to think creatively and share a part of themselves that sometimes gets lost at school.

Arts Integration and Social-Emotional Learning

Art evokes emotion. When you hear a song that was popular during your years in middle school, you are immediately transported into the school's smelly gym, full of awkward students at a Friday night dance. Or you see a photograph from your favorite restaurant and remember the smell wafting from the amazing meal you shared with friends that night. A painting can elicit a feeling of joy as you remember seeing that same view on a vacation with loved ones.

The link between art and emotions can help students make connections to what they are learning. A former middle school principal, Augustine Emuwa, calls these connections "landmarks" (personal communication, February 7, 2024). These are pivotal experiences that students have when their brain is still forming and that they can connect with harder, deeper learning. As the neural pathways strengthen during adolescent development, these multisensory landmarks broaden students' ability to remember what they have learned and to see it as meaningful. As a teacher, it may be hard to know exactly what those landmarks are for students, especially as they differ for each person; but exploring those moments can make a real difference in supporting students' learning and their emotional attachment to the curriculum. One way to see what is sticking is to have students reflect on something that they remember from class the day before, especially if you did something more arts or sensory based. Once you understand their thinking, you can continue to bring the learning back to those examples throughout the unit and potentially integrate new ones.

Giving students a lot of opportunities to engage in arts-based thinking allows them to better understand what will fit their social-emotional needs and how those needs connect to their learning. Educators need to be intentional about creating those social-emotional contexts in their lessons. This intentionality and exposure to a variety of opportunities to process their emotions through art are critical for students' development. Brooklyn Raney, founder of One Trusted Adult, talks about the importance of designing not just lessons but experiences for students. And in those experiences, she emphasizes the need for educators to incorporate *presence, play,* and *possibility* (personal communication, February 2, 2024). What I love about incorporating these three ideas into planning is that it gives all educators a way to think about the arc of learning in their classroom and what that means for engaging students using the components and strategies that are often more present in an arts-based classroom than in a more traditional classroom. For example, looking back at Figure 1.1, arts-based classrooms often use the action cycle (encountering, tinkering, choosing, practicing, and contributing) and the reflection cycle (describing, evaluating, connecting, envisioning, and integrating), which lead to students developing agency and a more integrated identity, meaning they are making decisions that are consistent with their values, beliefs, and goals (Farrington et al., 2019).

For Raney, *presence* means affirming a student's existence by checking in, which can be done through a question that they discuss with a partner or a whole-class check-in on how students are feeling. Inviting that student voice during the first five minutes of class makes it much more likely that students will stay engaged and continue to exercise their voice for the rest of their time in the classroom (Chandler, 2017).

Play in the classroom, collaborative or competitive, causes a heightened sense of emotion that can make an experience more memorable. It unlocks a part of the brain that can lead to one of those landmark moments that connect to deeper learning. Therefore, incorporating play isn't just about "fun"; it's actually a way to enhance learning while building relationships, connection, and shared experiences. Giving students the opportunity to get out of their seats, move around, act something out, and express themselves is important both for engaging them and for attaching muscle memory to the ability to remember the concept in the future. Play could be something as simple as acting out a vocabulary word to a partner in a game of Pictionary, creating a graffiti wall of questions, or performing a skit to teach the class a concept. One of Raney's favorite examples of this type of play is a game of "heads or tails" to review for a test. Students put their hands on their heads if they think the statement is true or on their "tails" if they think it's false. These types of games bring fun to the classroom, along with opportunities for students to take risks and have those landmark moments to attach learning to.

The concept of *possibility* embraces a look toward the future. This could look like asking about what students want to be able to do in the next month or next year, or what they hope tomorrow looks like. This forward thinking helps students to connect their learning to their dreams for the future and, as Raney says, lets young people know that we want to see them tomorrow, that we want to see their progress, and that their goals are possible to achieve (personal communication, February 2, 2024).

Throughout history we have seen young people process joy and sorrow through artistic expression both on their own and alongside others. After a traumatic experience, young people often are given paper and writing implements to express their feelings. Emuwa shared an experience from his time as a middle school principal when a young person at his school passed away during the school year (personal communication, February 7, 2024). The students couldn't believe that someone of or near their own age was suddenly gone. As he and his team worked to help students and staff process the tragedy, he drew upon his own experiences as a middle schooler when he found power in expressing himself through art and having a platform to display his understanding of the world. He worked to figure out how to bring that feeling to his students who were struggling. In reflecting on this experience, he said, "We made sure that kids had opportunities to do paintings, to do writings that we put in boxes, to make sure that they had ability to do little writings on strips." He described "symbolic gestures that just cemented this girl's existence" in an unforgettable way. The school conducted a full day of remembrance featuring a spoken-word poet, students sharing their artistic expressions, and a community remembrance in the form of a balloon release. As he said in our conversation, "Wherever those things fell at in the world, hopefully somebody got a whiff and got a taste of what these kids were experiencing and what they wanted to give their friend as a final goodbye." Though this is a sad story, it is also a beautiful one that shows the importance of art, social-emotional learning, and caring for one another in a public and authentic way.

Things to Keep in Mind

- **Allow time for processing.** All students have things in their life that are difficult to process and to understand. Giving them time to express those emotions, whether about an event in your community, your school, or the world, is important. The symbolism that can accompany these types of experiences can be both a landmark and a moment when students understand that they are seen and that their feelings matter.
- **Find moments for joy.** Giving students the opportunity to express themselves and have fun can be what makes learning stick. Designing joyful classroom experiences can also give you and your students a way to connect to one another.

Using Arts-Based Strategies for Creative Thinking and Problem Solving

Opening a classroom to creative problem solving leads to many different opportunities for students to share their learning and thinking. I saw in my own classroom, and have heard from teachers I work with, that many students are so afraid of being wrong that they avoid even attempting to do a problem or raising their hand. Their hope is that someone will just give them the answer or at least tell them exactly where to look. Infusing a classroom with more arts-based learning and creative problem solving can help students feel that they are free to take risks and that there can be multiple ways to get to the answer.

Math teacher Dora Medina acknowledged the importance of creative problem solving by having students talk through an open-ended problem with peers and figure out the solution without a lot of specific direction (personal communication, October 20, 2023). She has found that giving students the opportunity "to have a talk about math or just have a math discussion without really giving them guidance" can be one of the most effective ways to engage them. She said she sometimes gives her students "open-ended questions... or something else that might spark their creativity and give them space to have a conversation and for them to share their ideas out loud, to add on to each other's ideas, disagree, and agree, and to compare their thinking." As this observation suggests, open-ended questions can lead to many different possible answers, explanations, and a deeper understanding of the concept.

Meredith Kachel echoed this idea of creative problem solving when she shared that the best way she has ever engaged students in her art classes "is to instill quite a bit of trust in them in the art room" (personal communication, November 20, 2023). She notes that "kids,... especially middle schoolers,... don't like being handheld.... They are really gunning for that independence." As an example, she describes giving students scissors and lots of cardboard, along with access to Exacto knives that she keeps at her desk. She tells them that, working in teams, they can make whatever they want. Then she tells them, "'When you figure it out and you and your team are working on it, you may use the Exacto knives.' That gets them very excited, and all of a sudden, they start thinking about 'What are these things I'm going to make?' I found that the best way to engage kids is to give them some sort of responsibility or independence." She explains this type of thinking to her students as "exercising" as they would in a PE class, but instead of exercising their bodies, they are exercising their ability to creatively work through a problem. Trust, independence, responsibility, and self-expression are all things that middle grade students crave. Teachers may find it uncomfortable to share power in this way, but ultimately, doing so can lead to stronger developmental relationships in which students can take the lead and feel like their ideas are taken seriously (Search Institute, 2020).

Another way to include arts-based thinking in your classroom is through team-building activities. Examples include having teams compete to construct the tallest structure using marshmallows and toothpicks or the tallest tower using boxes that will withstand the teacher's attempt to blow the tower down; creating a mural that shows the individual and collective identity of the class; and playing the "human knot" game, in which students in a circle reach across to join hands with another person and then try to unravel the knot without letting go. These kinds of activities serve a dual purpose in that they build community in the classroom and allow for students to collaborate, take risks, and work together to solve a problem. If done more frequently than just at the beginning of the year, they can translate into other more content-specific learning experiences by allowing students to practice collaborative skills before embarking on a challenging topic, project, or concept.

These examples show how creative thinking and problem solving give students the responsibility they crave and the freedom to take risks and to figure out new ways of doing things. They also give students the experience of being a part of a group of their peers, working together to solve a problem.

Things to Keep in Mind

- **Have a few open-ended questions in your back pocket to foster arts-based thinking.** These are all questions that don't necessarily have a correct answer and can lead to a robust discussion and even debate. They also can be used for almost any topic or content area:
  - Which one doesn't belong?
  - How do these things connect?
  - What else could be added to this list?
  - How is it similar or different?
  - How can you prove that this statement is true (or false)?
  - What choices could this person make?
- **Community building is important year-round.** Most teachers start with intentional community building at the beginning of the year but then, after the first week or two, jump into the curriculum without looking back. It's important to remember that classroom dynamics change throughout the year, and students need structured time to practice working together and using new skills they have acquired over the course of the school year. Incorporating small opportunities to creatively problem solve together will make for deeper learning.
- **Trust your students but maintain boundaries.** As was evident in Kachel's art classroom, she gave her students parameters before allowing them to use tools that require more trust. Sharing power and allowing students more responsibility is important in middle school, but just as important is for them to understand your expectations and the classroom boundaries. Make sure to review classroom agreements and your expectations and objectives

before giving students the freedom to be creative in their problem solving.

Using Art in the Curriculum

What do you see? What do you hear? How does this make you feel? These are questions that students of varying levels of understanding and background knowledge are able to engage with in a classroom. They are also questions, like the open-ended questions listed earlier, that don't necessarily have a specific right or wrong answer.

In my social studies class, I loved using photographs, songs, political cartoons, and paintings to introduce and then immerse students in the time period we were learning about and to engage them through a natural curiosity in their community, as well as to help them empathize and look at multiple perspectives. For example, to introduce our immigration unit, I used a song that students analyzed to think about the themes of chasing dreams, freedom, and what it means to be "home." Reflecting on memorable lessons in middle school, one of my former students said, "In 7th grade, I remember listening to the song 'Home' by Dierks Bentley and analyzing it, and after all of these years it's like a core memory for me." As a teacher you never know what is going to click for your students, but giving them the opportunity to find an opening into what they are learning and a landmark to return to is instrumental in engaging them.

There are some important things to consider when you are choosing the art to use in your classroom, particularly for teaching about what can be called "hard history." To help guide teachers' thinking in this area, the organization Learning for Justice (n.d.) suggests the following practices:

- Connect to the present.
- Know how to talk about hard topics, such as race and racism.
- Educate to realize power.
- Reveal the unseen.
- Resist telling a simple story.

Let's look at each of these more closely.

Connect to the present. This means making connections to the past and exploring how it has shaped present-day society. Helping students to explore and apply their knowledge of the past makes them better equipped to take what they have learned and use it now and in the future.

Know how to talk about hard topics, such as race and racism. Make sure to set clear guidelines for whatever discussion you are going to have. Bring students into that process and discuss what would make them feel safe in expressing their thoughts and opinions. In Chapter 3, we talked about students giving one another feedback. You could use a similar process to engage students in a conversation about what it looks like to discuss difficult topics. This doesn't mean that you shouldn't have these hard conversations; instead, make sure to be transparent about the guardrails for how the conversation will take place.

Educate to realize power. Critical thinking and the ability to ask questions should be a part of any curriculum. Help students look for the underlying stories and how those can complicate the conventional stories that have been told.

Reveal the unseen. In Chapter 3, we looked at the importance of storytelling. Revealing the unseen is a way of sharing the stories of those who aren't often talked about or deepening the understanding of those who are. Testimonies and hearing people share about their own experience helps students to better understand the thoughts, experiences, and motivations of people throughout history.

Resist telling a simple story. Students should learn the realities of our history, and really about any topic, in a way that is age appropriate and culturally responsive—meaning that you are incorporating and centering the uniqueness of your students' experiences and identities (National Equity Project, n.d.). The story should not present a single perspective but instead show complexity and differing perspectives. Depending on the topic, it can also be connected to a global view. Complicating the narrative helps students to dig beyond the headlines and critically think about the issues (Learning for Justice, n.d.).

Analyzing Propaganda

As a social studies teacher, one of the most important things that I felt I could do was to teach my students to be media literate and to help them to understand that the art around them was one way to do that. Given the 24/7 news cycle, the rise of artificial intelligence (AI), and the overwhelming number of notifications from social media, students need to be able to discern fact from fiction and to know where the information is coming from and the message that the source is attempting to convey. Starting with the 1754 political cartoon featuring a snake and a "Join, or Die" caption, and progressing to World War I and II posters, cartoons, and movies, and finally to modern-day propaganda, my students had the opportunity to analyze and better understand the objectives and appeals being used to inform, persuade, and call people to action. This type of art can be a powerful entry point for students, especially if you start with observational questions and build to analysis. Here are examples of questions that follow this progression:

- Observation
  - What do you see? (List colors, objects, people, or places.)
  - What words or phrases appear in the image? (List them below.)
  - What actions are taking place?
- Digging in
  - Who created the image, and, if known, in what year?
  - Which of the objects, people, or places symbolize something?
  - What does each symbol represent?
  - Of the words you identified in the observation list, which do you think are the most significant? Why?
- Meaning
  - What emotion is this image trying to evoke?
  - What tools did the artist use to evoke those emotions?
  - What message is being conveyed?
  - What was taking place at this time in history that made this piece important to create?

Because propaganda appears in so many places, this questioning strategy can be used in almost any classroom. In science, you could have students look at how businesses talk about climate change versus how activists talk about it, or how car manufacturers are selling their newest technology in EV or hybrid cars. You could then have students look at the science behind these technologies and analyze how truthful these different groups are in conveying their message. In math, students could look at the statistics that are used to support the claims in propaganda and analyze them for accuracy and for how they are being used to persuade or manipulate one side or another. In all areas, it is vitally important for students to know how to dig into the things that they are seeing and to not take them at face value or react based on the initial emotional response that often comes with seeing this type of art.

How to bring this to your classroom

1. Gather ads, cartoons about society, and posters about a topic you are studying. Make sure you are intentional and thoughtful in choosing these images. If you find a provocative image that you think is important to share, clarify and be transparent as to why you are choosing that particular image and what your goal is in having students analyze it. The same holds true for photographs. The goal should never be "shock and awe." If you decide the image is something that is valuable to share, think about how long students will be looking at the image, how big the image is, and, if it is in video format, whose voice is narrating about the image and the impact it had on society.

2. Teach students about the tools and strategies used to persuade audiences, including the following:

   - Appealing to people's emotions and identity
   - Telling half-truths
   - Calling people names or using stereotypes
   - Demonizing a side or a group of people
   - Generalizing a complex issue
   - Using a slogan that catches people's attention
   - Using well-known or powerful symbols
   - Using humor

   Helping students to understand the different elements used in propaganda to persuade throughout history can help them be able to recognize these tools and strategies

in modern-day propaganda and speak out against mis- and disinformation. For the first three strategies in the list, be careful that through your lesson you are not reinforcing stereotypes or demonizing a group.
3. Have students analyze propaganda from multiple perspectives and sources using the questions listed earlier to observe, dig in, and make meaning by identifying the tools and objectives used by the creator of the propaganda.
4. Then have students reflect on the impact of the propaganda they were analyzing, along with how propaganda influences the greater society today and has done so throughout history.
5. After analyzing propaganda in any content area, you can also have students use that knowledge to create their own propaganda and then explain why they created what they did, the tools they used, and how they think it would have affected people's perceptions. This is another powerful way for students to use art to share their learning and assess their understanding of audiences, tools, and effective communication of a message.

Analyzing Images

Like those that appear in propaganda, images that are not used for that purpose can be an important entry point for students. In Naomi Wilfred's classroom, she used to start with what she called "wonder images" (personal communication, December 8, 2023). She would put up an image and ask students to share what they wondered about related to the image. Once students had a list of "wonderings," Wilfred would send them off to find the answers to their questions. This activity gave them the opportunity to choose some aspect of what they were learning and to become an expert in something new to share with the class. A similar activity asks students to finish statements that start with "I think, I notice, and I wonder" to spark that mindset of creative thinking and problem solving.

To help students develop the ability to understand the power of perspective, you could start with a very zoomed-in view of an image related to whatever you are studying and ask students what they think it is. As you zoom out, students then learn the important skill of revising their predictions and rethinking their initial thoughts. This approach is a low-stakes way to help students take risks and continue to learn how to ask additional questions before coming to a conclusion.

Activities such as these contribute to the building of community in the classroom. They also keep students in a state of curiosity and questioning.

Another way to use images is to have students create a story based on an image. One of my former students reflected on a story that I had students write using an image from Chris Van Allsburg's *The Mysteries of Harris Burdick*. In her reflection, she said that her story was one of the best she had ever written because it was based on a picture that she had chosen, and she had been allowed to write it with little guidance aside from having to use the one line that served as a title for the picture. She said that even though she didn't like writing stories, she found this experience enjoyable. Just the simple act of giving students a choice of image, a line to incorporate, and the freedom to be creative resulted in some incredibly imaginative stories and many different interpretations of the same images.

Opening class with students finding a meme to represent how they are feeling can give you information about what thoughts they are bringing into class that day. Similarly, asking them to write a caption on an image to make a meme about something that you are studying can inform you as to what they understand about the topic. In a science class, imagine showing a cartoon image of a white blood cell and a red blood cell and then having students write a funny dialogue between them to discuss their relationship; or during a geometry unit, giving students an image that shows different types of shapes and having them reflect on how the shapes are related. As you can see, using images as teaching tools is a strategy that can be used in any content area.

How to bring this to your classroom

1. Identify images that will spark curiosity in your students and connect to what they are learning.
2. Share the image with a specific prompt that will teach or review a concept or help students reflect. This could come in the form of sentence prompts such as these:
    - I think, I notice, I wonder...
    - This image connects to what we learned because...
    - When I see this image, I feel...
    - This image reminds me of...
    - From my perspective, I think this image...
    - Who? What? When? Where? Why?

3. Have students share their thinking using any of the following methods:
    - A dyad conversation in which one student in the pair shares their thoughts for one or two minutes while the other just listens, and then they switch roles. This activity allows students to practice active listening and to make sure that each person has an equal opportunity to share their thoughts without judgment.

- Small groups, in which each student shares one aspect of the image that sticks out to them.
- A silent, written class "conversation" recorded on a large sheet of paper or on an online platform where students can add to one another's thoughts.
- A whole-class conversation in which each student shares one word or phrase about the image.

4. To incorporate image analysis into a more complex assignment, you can ask students to write a story about the image, as described in the assignment based on Chris Van Allsburg's book, or to create an image to teach a concept or reflect on something they learned.

Analyzing Photographs

As illustrated in the opening of this chapter and the example of the Harlem Renaissance, I often used photographs to help students gain a deeper understanding of a particular time period. Looking at Jacob Riis's photos of tenement houses in the 1890s or Dorothea Lange's photographs of the Dust Bowl during the 1930s gave students a glimpse into people's lives during that time and the opportunity to think about purpose, message, and audience to answer questions as to why these particular photos were taken. As with propaganda, I would start our analysis of photographs with the observational questions (What do you see?) and move to the more in-depth ones (What impact do you think this photo had on people at the time?). We would then study the time period and what was happening, the effect of people highlighting these glimpses of people's lives through photographs, and what the eventual outcomes were for people then and today. These types of photographs can help build empathy and allow students to see themselves, their friends, or their families in the photo, giving them the ability to better understand what people were possibly feeling. Photographs can also be used to introduce students to unfamiliar concepts and ideas or even people, places, and things that can lead to more questions and deeper learning. Many students have not had the opportunity to travel to other states, countries, or even sometimes out of their neighborhood. Using photographs to introduce other people, places, and cultures makes the world come alive in a way that words on a page often can't.

How to bring this to your classroom

1. Find photographs that illustrate the concept that your students are studying. As with propaganda, take time to be intentional and thoughtful about the images you use in class. Make sure to give enough context before sharing photos that may evoke strong emotions. Photographs are a powerful teaching tool but need to be treated with the intentionality and humanity they deserve.
2. Have students analyze the photographs using questions such as these:

- What do you see in the photograph?
- What is happening in the photograph?
- What emotion is conveyed by this photograph?
    - If it is a photograph of people, what are their facial expressions? What does their body language tell you?
    - What colors appear in the photograph? How do they influence the emotion portrayed?
- Who took the photograph?
- When was the picture taken?
- Why do you think this photograph was taken?

- What impact do you think this photograph had on people when it was taken? What impact does it have today?
3. After analyzing the photographs, students could do any of the following:

    - Share their analysis with one another to understand multiple perspectives and test their assumptions.
    - If known, study the backstory of the photograph to better understand the context of a time period or event and see how their analysis did or didn't match what the photographer was intending.
    - Create a timeline by arranging photographs in a specific order, using their understanding of the events portrayed. Photographs can also be used to create timelines to show causes and effects of a natural disaster or a progression of a phenomenon in nature in a science class. Having students look at photos and put them in order or use them to explain a concept can help to dispel misunderstandings and lead to better understanding.

4. As an extension activity, have students take their own photographs using techniques they saw in the photographs they were analyzing. They can share these in class and see how their classmates' analysis matches their intention in taking the photograph.

Incorporating Music

Almost every middle schooler I know has a playlist of hundreds of songs that play on repeat through their earbuds or headphones. From the "oldies" that their parents listen to or that they heard on social media, to the newest song from a current artist, music is something that spans generations.

Incorporating music into the classroom can happen in a variety of ways. Wilfred believes that "music in general just needs to be a part of every classroom culture.... Are you playing music in the morning? Are you having students create their own playlist? Are you having students tell you what songs they want and... adding [them] to the classroom playlist?" (personal communication, December 8, 2023). Taking student suggestions for a classroom playlist can build a culture of student voice, along with a stronger community and sense of belonging as students hear the songs they requested being played and enjoyed by their classmates. Music can also evoke emotion and change the mood of a classroom. A high-energy song can help prepare students for a busy day, and a more peaceful selection can help create a relaxed mindset for a stressful day.

If you don't want to have a general-purpose class playlist, you can create one that is connected to the time period or topic being studied. For example, playing songs by Ella Fitzgerald or Louis Armstrong to introduce a unit on the origins of jazz is much more effective than a lecture alone. Learning about the fight for rights using protest songs throughout history is an effective way to show students the power of using one's voice and how that voice can be elevated through music.

You can also use music that has been purposely created to tie to the curriculum and make content easier to remember. Both of my children still sing a song about the Euphrates River that they learned in 6th grade social studies. By the end of that unit, we all knew the words and how it connected to their study of Mesopotamia. My brothers can still sing the song "Fifty Nifty United States" that they learned in middle school, and my husband often embarrasses our kids with his version of the Animaniacs' "Preposition Song." And at some point in our schooling, we probably all watched the animated rendition of the song "I'm Just a Bill," which I also showed my own students when we studied the long process of a bill becoming a law in the United States.

Another favorite activity, which can even be used as a form of assessment, is having students create a playlist to show their understanding of a concept or a novel. As part of their study of a novel, students might pick a song for each chapter to show the arc of the story, or they could select a "walk-up song" for each character. As they reflect on why they chose the song, you can assess understanding and see how they are connecting meaning to the piece of writing. Playlists can also reveal how students are feeling. During the pandemic, the schools that I worked with had students create a playlist that represented how they felt from March 2020 to March 2021. Their reflections explaining their choices revealed their swings of emotions, from being happy about being home for an extended break, to boredom, to fear, to an uncertainty about what was happening, and then a combination of apprehension and happiness as school began to open again. Tying music to difficult concepts, emotions, and processes can give students that landmark to attach their learning to.

How to bring this to your classroom

1. If you aren't able to play music in the classroom, remember that song lyrics, like photographs and propaganda, can be analyzed for tools used, meaning, and context. For example, in a poetry unit, my students brought in songs that had examples of metaphors, similes, onomatopoeia, and rhyme schemes. We didn't always listen to the songs in class, but students enjoyed seeing the music they were listening to in a different light and how what we were learning was applied by their favorite artists.

2. If you are creating a class playlist or having students create their own for classroom sharing, make sure that the songs are "clean" versions and that you listen to them to ensure that they are appropriate for a school setting. For class playlists, you can post an online form where students can request songs or do a monthly call for new songs to add to the list. Asking students to create their own playlists for a project is a great way to collect songs that mean something to them. If you have students contribute to a playlist, make sure to have plenty of opportunities for listening to that playlist so students hear their contributions.
3. If you are collecting songs from a particular time period, make sure to include a variety of perspectives and identities. See it as a great opportunity to share the voices of people who may not always be highlighted.

Incorporating Film

Like the other art forms we have explored in this chapter, film can be used in a variety of ways. Today's students are often watching short films to get their news and to understand the world around them. And, as with so many other forms of art, students need to understand how to be able to analyze a film and recognize the tools that filmmakers are using to engage their audience.

Across the content areas, film can immerse students in a particular place and time. In social studies, I often used films from or about a specific time period to explore the topic in a different way. From news conferences to speeches to documentaries, these films captured the attention of my students in a way that my explanation or the written curriculum couldn't. As I did for other forms of art, I had students analyze the films for audience, purpose, tools being used, and how they could be used to convey a message in a unique way. Films could show students an area of the world that they had never visited or an animal habitat they were studying. Whatever the topic, talking about what is filmed and what is not, how the subjects of the film are portrayed, and why the film was produced are all important pieces of using film in a classroom.

Film can also be used to help explain a difficult concept. I love this example from a friend on the creative use of film in an English classroom. She remembers a lesson on the concept of plot in which the teacher used the movie *Charade*, with Cary Grant and Audrey Hepburn. As she recalls, "Each character had an icon, and each activity had a different icon that we had to graph. We moved the characters and activities into good, bad, and questionable columns as the movie progressed. We made predictions about the ending of the movie after each class period—we were always wrong!" Although the teacher could have relied only on a book or a short story to teach the concept of plot, using a film made this a particularly compelling and memorable lesson.

How to bring this to your classroom

1. Keep your eyes open for films that can help students make stronger connections to their learning and enhance their understanding. You never know when you will see something in a film—whether it's a one-minute clip or a full-length production, a cartoon, a current box-office hit, or a classic movie—that will help illuminate a concept in your classroom.
2. As with the other forms of visual media, make sure you are intentional about the films you choose and think

about who is telling the story and how the concepts are portrayed. Be sure the selection is age appropriate and culturally responsive.
3. Before watching a film, tell students to look for ways the filmmakers are using tools such as the ones identified in the propaganda section of this chapter or techniques such as camera angles, point of view, lighting, close-ups, perspective, and other elements of cinematography intended to capture their audience.
4. After watching the film, discuss the tools and techniques students saw and how they affected their understanding of the concepts or time period. Making students aware of these tools and their possible effects can help them better understand how to analyze what they are watching and what is influencing them in their daily lives.

Things to Keep in Mind

- **Start small.** Find one or two places where art can be integrated into your curriculum. For example, you might start class by playing a song that connects to the topic you will be covering. Or begin with a picture to activate students' thinking and engage them in conversations with one another.
- **Have students find examples.** Give students an opportunity to contribute and share examples of art throughout history or pieces that represent something you are teaching about. This is a good way for students to show their understanding and see that their input has value.
- **Help students transfer their newly acquired skills in observation and analysis.** Give students multiple, frequent opportunities to use their new knowledge to

better understand the art they see around them. The more you can connect what they are learning to what they see and hear, the more they will understand the art-enriched world they live in.

Art as an Assessment

Giving students the opportunity to create art outside the art classroom can make for a memorable learning experience. It allows students to see the value in using many different modalities to show their learning and enables them to use their creativity to connect to their community in new and different ways. As a social studies teacher, I had many opportunities to use art to excite students' natural curiosity about the world.

One example of integrating art into the curriculum that was memorable for many of my former students was a "rights collage" project. After learning about civil rights, women's rights, consumers' rights, workers' rights, voters' rights, and children's rights, I asked my students to create a collage in the physical shape of something that represented the fight for rights, from flappers to ballot boxes, and then fill one side with pictures and words that represented all the different groups and the rights and reforms that were gained, while the other was decorated to represent the physical shape it was in. They then wrote a short paper explaining how their collage represented the rights and reforms that we learned about and how those reforms still affect life today. As one student said, "I learned about my great-grandma, history, and loved the art project." Another, whose project was based on a 1920s flapper, liked the assignment "because it was not a boring project for me, and I could be creative with it."

Another assignment that gave students the opportunity to flex their artistic muscle was an 8th grade "throne project" in a unit on Greek mythology. In this project, after learning about the 12 gods and goddesses of Mount Olympus and their influence on Greek culture, students created their own god or goddess identity and a 3-D model of their throne; they also chose an appropriate symbol and animal related to their newly formed identity. In a short paper, they were asked to answer the following questions:

- What are you the god/goddess of? Why?
- What is your throne made of? Why did you choose that material?
- What kind of cloth are you sitting on? Why did you choose that material?
- What is your symbol? How does this symbol connect to your power?
- What is your animal? How does this animal connect to your power?
- What are two decorations related to your power?
- What are you responsible for in human life? How will you influence society?

Reflecting on this project, one former student said, "I have always loved crafts and being creative, so when this cross-curricular project was handed to me, I had the best time letting my mind run wild and being able to physically create the idea that I had written about!" This project not only allowed for the use of art but also tied to middle schoolers' inherent search for identity in who they are and who they want to be.

Social studies is not the only subject area where an arts-based assessment can be incorporated. In a unit on geometry, students could use what they have learned to create a sculpture that is balanced, includes symmetry, and incorporates different types of angles. They could also analyze a work of art, looking for and calculating those same concepts. In a unit on algebra, students could create art using the golden ratio and the Fibonacci sequence or find those elements in other works of art. One of my favorite places in the Museum of Science and Industry in Chicago is the Numbers in Nature exhibit, with its mirror maze and opportunities to see patterns including logarithmic spirals, fractal branching, the golden ratio, and the Voronoi pattern in nature. Using these concepts, students could create their own patterns showing their understanding of equations, scale, and proportions.

Teachers at a school in Chicago based an interdisciplinary science/art project on the Golden Records carried by two NASA *Voyager* spacecrafts launched in 1977. The phonograph records contain a wide variety of sounds and images of everyday life on Earth, intended as time capsules that could be found by life forms that might exist elsewhere in the universe. In this project, the teachers had students think about what sound bites they would share with beings from another planet to explain where and who they (the students) are. The students decorated golden records with images and recorded actual sounds from their day-to-day life to answer the question "What impact do you want to show the universe that we had?" As the art teacher and lead on this project explained, Kachel was amazed by what students captured, how they gave life to this project, and how interesting it was to hear what they heard every day (personal communication, November 20, 2023). Similarly, another teacher reflected on her own experience in 8th grade, when her English class created a 10-year time capsule after spending weeks gathering materials, pictures, decorations, and responses to prompts. She then watched 10 years later as people opened the capsules and shared their findings on social media. Reflecting on why she remembered this particular project, the teacher said, "I think the translation into something tangible was REALLY what did it for me."

These examples represent a variety of subject areas and components, but they have an important element in common. Each instilled a sense of pride and ownership in students as they created something that showed their identity, their learning, and their place in the community.

How to bring this to your classroom

1. Review your current assessments. Ask yourself the following questions:

   - What am I trying to assess?
   - How am I currently assessing those areas?
   - Can I assess what I'm hoping to in a variety of ways that allow students choice in sharing their learning?
   - Does my current assessment offer an opportunity for student choice and creativity?

2. Find one assessment where you can add a more creative option. You could replace your current assessment with this new option or give students a choice between the two.

3. Once students have turned in their assessment, gather feedback about what they liked and disliked about it, and have them reflect on what they learned. This feedback will help you to refine the assessment and understand other ways you could incorporate artistic options in the future.

Things to Keep in Mind

- **Assessments can come in all shapes and sizes.** Giving students the opportunity to express their learning in a variety of ways can lead to some impressive outcomes across the curriculum. Designing a dream car or a rocket that can fly, performing in a poetry slam, writing and having a platform to share an original rap or a skit with friends, performing in a concert to help raise awareness for a cause, creating a collage—these are all assessments of learning that stuck with people far past their middle school years. They may not be what people traditionally think of when they think of an assessment, but the lessons from these projects stayed with them far longer than a traditional test did.

Learning Stations

One of the most effective ways I infused art into my classroom was through learning stations. Learning stations are often used in early grades but then phased out as students get older, even though, as we saw in Chapter 1, older students are often more able to take control of their learning and really want that independence and trust to work through a topic on their own.

I used learning stations in a variety of ways. Sometimes they were one- or two-day experiences on a specific topic, such as music and art from the 1960s or propaganda during World War II. Other times, work at learning stations would span a week or two. What students loved about stations is that they could work at their own pace, collaborate and problem solve with their peers, and explore the topics in whatever order made sense to them. Because these stations often centered around different forms of art, students also had the opportunity to analyze, interpret, and create meaning in creative ways.

One example of this type of learning took place during our study of the Great Depression. In this set of learning stations, students had seven different activities to complete, covering a variety of topics. They could start in any order and use the artifacts—many of them photos, poems, cartoons, or songs—to answer questions or create their own art to reflect their learning.

In one of the stations, students used maps, charts, and graphs to look at shifts in population and crop harvests during the years of the Great Depression. In another, students looked at statistics related to wages and prices in 1932 and were asked to determine how much it might cost to make a cake and what percent of a person's typical salary it would take to celebrate a special occasion, compared to today. In a third station, students mapped the effects of the Dust Bowl on farmers. The stations helped to create context and an understanding of what was happening during this time period.

The rest of the stations integrated a form of art to allow students to hear the voices or see the people that they were learning about, dramatizing through sound and sight what it was like to live during the 1930s. In one station, students were asked to analyze political cartoons that showed the many issues Franklin Roosevelt would be dealing with as he entered his presidency, the hurdles of passing and implementing the New Deal, and the effects of different solutions or events on Americans. In another, students were asked to listen to a song from the Great Depression and illustrate the content of what they were hearing. Songs such as "Brother, Can You Spare a Dime," "I'm Going Down the Road Feeling Bad," and "Collector Man Blues" enabled my students to explore the feelings and experiences expressed through the lyrics and performances of the artists who wrote and sang them. Students also had the opportunity to analyze Dorothea Lange's photographs, read letters written to First Lady Eleanor Roosevelt, analyze poetry written from a variety of perspectives, and listen to sound recordings of speeches and interviews. Each of these formats brought students into the time period in a way that a textbook could not. The art gave them an entry point into people's lives, their celebrations, and their struggles.

Learning through art can be translated into a variety of content areas. The thing to keep in mind is that students need enough structure to be successful, meaningful feedback in the moment to make sure they are on the right track, and a timeline that allows for everyone to complete the core learning.

How to bring this to your classroom

1. Find a concept or unit in which collaboration and work at stations will deepen the learning for your students.
2. Prepare students by teaching the background information of the topic so they have some knowledge before jumping into independent learning.
3. To keep things manageable, try to have no more than four students per station. This will mean that you need to have enough stations in your classroom to accommodate all of your students. This could mean having multiple sets of the same station, or it could mean having enough different activities for groups to be working on all different stations at the same time.
4. Make sure you explicitly teach students how to move from one station to the next and what they need to do in order to have their station work considered successfully

completed. This completion may require checking in with you or answering a check-out question.
5. Make the stations diverse by including different activities and ways to show learning. If at one station students are analyzing a form of art, then have them create something or write a personal reflection about a piece of art at the next station.
6. Once students finish the station work, debrief their learning and understanding as a class. Make sure to tie the stations to the background knowledge that you presented earlier and to what the class will be working on next.

Things to Keep in Mind

- **Not every unit is conducive to this type of learning.** Learning stations are a format that you may use only a couple of times a year or for shorter intervals during a unit. In my classroom, we did two sets of stations lasting a couple of weeks and five or six that lasted a couple of days. If you want to do this type of learning, consider units that include reflective elements or areas with open-ended responses to prompts. Having these opportunities for learning with their peers and at their own pace gave my students the chance to learn skills in time management, collaboration, and responsibility, alongside the content.
- **A good management system is important.** Planning for this type of learning takes time. You need to figure out where you are going to store the materials students need for the stations (in folders, online, in boxes), how students will move from station to station (do the stations move or do the students?), and how you will assess learning for each station. One mistake I made when I first started

teaching was waiting until the end to assess all the stations at once. The grading took me days, and students didn't get prompt feedback. After a few years, I realized that it was more efficient to assess their learning with them as they finished each station. They could then go back and make corrections if needed and had the opportunity to share their thinking in real time.

- **Potential resources are everywhere.** I found things to add to my stations in many places I went. In visiting museums, I found new examples of artwork or photographs to include. Through podcasts I would find a new speech or poem to share. Sometimes a student would share something they found that would make its way into a learning station. You never know where inspiration will come from!
- **Students who finish quickly will need additional learning opportunities.** Organize the stations so that most are devoted to the core learning that you want all students to attain and a few others feature extensions of learning. For example, you might have eight stations, but only six are part of the core experience, while the last two go beyond the core. Alternatively, you could have students choose one of the learning stations as a focus for more research or have them create an additional piece of art or even an additional learning station based on that research if they finish the core learning ahead of schedule.

Wrapping It Up

As actor Harvey Fierstein (2012) has said, "Art has the power to transform, to illuminate, to educate, inspire and motivate" (para. 12). In researching for this book, I was amazed, but not completely surprised, by the number of people I communicated with who mentioned art in their memories of middle school. Watching my own children interact with art every day and seeing the influence that it has in their world, I realize that it makes sense that students would remember landmark moments when art was included in their learning. In a time when it is imperative that we teach students to be discerning about their surroundings and to be media literate, as well as give them opportunities to collaborate and express themselves, incorporating art is a powerful way to make all those things happen. Use the questions in Figure 4.1 to get started on using art to spark student interest.

FIGURE 4.1
Finding the SPARK for Arts Integration

Study—Where could you incorporate art or arts-based strategies into your units?

Pilot—How can you give students more opportunity to express themselves in their learning? What's one strategy you want to try?

Analyze—What data can you collect to know if students have a better understanding of the material when art or arts-based strategies have been incorporated?

Reflect—What are "landmark moments" that you noticed your students reacting positively to in your classroom?

Kindle—What are other ways you can incorporate big or small moments of arts-based thinking or creativity into your classroom?

5

Connecting Learning to Life Outside School

> *Education is the most powerful weapon we can use to change the world.*
>
> —Nelson Mandela

It's a Tuesday afternoon at the Mayne Stage in Rogers Park, a neighborhood in the North Side area of Chicago. Eighteen middle school students, two professional songwriters, and three teachers, including myself, are gathered for the students to record a song called "Shine a Light" to help raise money and awareness for the organization A Better Life for Kids, which supports children and families in Ghana. The students have been working for months with Wendy and DB, who are professional children's musicians, to first brainstorm the song lyrics and then practice for this important day. The excitement in the room is palpable as the students get ready to share their talent in such a meaningful way. Throughout the afternoon and into the early evening, the students record their parts, each of them growing stronger and more confident as they sing the solos and join the choruses they have been working on. As we celebrate on the stage at the end of the night, we are all excited to hear what the final product sounds like and to anticipate what type of reception it will receive when it is released into the world.

Making Connections

This is boring. When will I ever use this? How is this meaningful to my real life? These are the thoughts that often go through middle school students' heads as they sit in class. Sometimes they voice these thoughts out loud or in writing. Sometimes they express their feelings through their behavior.

How can I make this more meaningful to my students? How can I help them connect this concept, lesson, skill, or information to their life inside and outside school? How can I create the conditions in my classroom for them to realize why they need to understand this concept? These are the questions that often went through my head as a teacher as I planned new units or new ways to teach a lesson.

This disconnect between the assigned work and how students perceive that work can be frustrating for the teacher who has put a lot of time and effort into the lesson being presented. It's also frustrating for the student who is trying to make sense of the abstract skills or content that they are attempting to learn. Often this situation leads to a teacher responding to students' frustration by saying, "You'll need this one day—you'll see," or "It's on the test," or (with a big sigh) "Just do the work," assuming that the question is an avoidance tactic. Students then conclude that, like them, their teachers don't know why the work is necessary and that it's not meaningful. As we know from Chapter 1, this questioning of meaning from students is developmental and often emerges from curiosity and trying to understand the world around them. The more we can do as educators to support that motivation, the more students will be able to make connections between what they are learning and their life outside school.

How do we help build this relevancy for students? So far, we have looked at ways to collect data from students about their perceptions and co-create solutions with them, ways to infuse storytelling and identity into lessons, and ways to use the arts to help make meaningful connections. Now, in this chapter, we consider how to help students connect what they are learning to the outside world.

In an interview, Camille Farrington, senior advisor at the University of Chicago Consortium, discussed why it's so important to have time during the day for students to talk about life outside school, so that school is not entirely disconnected from what everybody else is talking about (personal communication, November 15, 2023). Without that time, school doesn't feel credible. And if no one is acknowledging or talking about what is happening or giving students opportunities to develop their own opinions and connections, then school starts to seem out of touch. Educator Naomi Wilfred reiterated this point when she stated that one of the most effective ways she found to engage her students was by using novels and historical events to "provide spaces to talk about real issues," such as defining boundaries, body image, consent, gender identity, and the effects on society of phrases like "boys will be boys" or the "talented tenth" (personal communication, December 8, 2023). These conversations led to an open space where both students and teachers, including Wilfred, could bring their full selves, and students could make connections between what they were learning and the world around them.

So much of what students remember from middle school are things that connect to their interests, to their future, or to situations where they felt that they made a lasting impact. They don't necessarily remember learning to write an essay, but they do remember having to write a letter to a congressperson about an issue they cared about or to the principal about something they wanted to see changed in the school using those same skills. They may not remember every element on the periodic table, but they do remember the magic of seeing the chemical reactions involved in making ice cream in their 7th grade science class.

In this chapter, using reflections from students, teachers, and other adults remembering their experiences in middle school, we look at practical ways to bring relevancy into the classroom using daily connections to life outside school, choice, relevant life skills, and service learning. From group work and finding reliable sources, to outdoor education trips, so much of what sticks with middle school students has to do with skills that will help them navigate the world around them—their friendships, the adults in their lives, and their everyday experiences.

Addressing the Call for "Intellectual Necessity"

Making learning more meaningful doesn't necessarily mean having to change your entire curriculum. Instead, it can mean connecting concepts students are learning to brief moments in their day or creating a need to understand a particular topic. Science teacher Cathy Gormley says she likes "to engage students in real-world phenomena," which, she notes, is a focus of the Next Generation Science Standards (personal communication, November 6, 2023). She tries to link her science units to students' home life as much as possible. She asks them, "Where have you seen chemistry before? And tell me how that looks in your own kitchen." She explains that at the start of the school year she "talked a lot about baking and cooking and food because everybody loves baking and cooking and food. The whole entire first unit, which is all about chemistry and chemical reactions, I would say, 'Give me an example of when you made breakfast this morning. What happened in the pan? Did it look like it did when you first started cooking it? What do you think happens in the oven? Give me an example of something that you make at home for your parents.'"

Gormley's approach demonstrates that this type of connection doesn't take a lot of time but does help a student who may not think science is something they are "good" at or something that is "relevant" to see how chemistry plays out in their everyday life. Gormley also mentioned that these small moments often provide a "bonus" by opening up opportunities for storytelling and building stronger relationships with students. Talking about the food their family eats sometimes leads to broader conversations about culture, as they describe, for example, the dish their Assyrian grandmother makes. "Sometimes we get off on a tangent.... 'What's in that dish? I want to try this.' It helps me build relationships with them, which is the foundation of my classroom management—connecting with the kids. I try to do that almost every day... and they have told me that they appreciate that. They feel like there's meaning behind what they're doing, and it's not just... one more fact to memorize or one more worksheet to fill out" (personal communication, November 6, 2023).

In my own social studies classes, I made these kinds of real-world connections by talking, for example, about the tools used in propaganda and then having students share places where they had seen these tools used online, on billboards, or in magazines. This led to lively discussions and students bringing in examples from all parts of their life. Or we would talk about the roots of democracy in ancient cultures, and they would begin the process of making the connections to how those same components of democracy show up in our government today.

Math classes offer many ways to make these connections. For example, math teacher Dora Medina described how she taught math fluency and the skill of writing math expressions using a problem in which, much like her students, a student goes to the corner store four days a week and spends $5 each time (personal communication, October 20, 2023). Medina's students had to write the expression and then, when they evaluated the resulting equation, they not only learned the math but also realized that many of them were spending $20 a week without even thinking about it! Other opportunities in math class could involve using fractions in a recipe and figuring out how to scale it to make enough for the entire class (with the option of having students actually prepare the recipe) or having students figure out groupings or scheduling for an upcoming field trip or special event at school.

A colleague reflecting on his time as a middle school student shared that his most memorable lesson was making a spreadsheet in order to calculate his grades. The lesson taught him how to create algorithms using a spreadsheet, which he still uses today, and how to use variables instead of numbers, which helped him be more successful in algebra. Because his learning had been embedded in a meaningful context, the process of creating algorithms stuck with him, and he was able to see how algebra could be used in other applications and was, in fact, a necessity.

Improvement coach Yekaterina Milvidskaia notes that recognizing this type of necessity is important to build relevancy for students, and teachers must create conditions in which students have a real need to know and understand the topic (personal communication, November 30, 2023). Mathematics professor Guershon Harel (2008) defines this concept as the Necessity Principle, which states, "For students to learn what we intend to teach them, they must have a need for it, where 'need' means intellectual need," not just a social or economic one (p. 900). Thus teachers must set up classroom learning conditions in which students understand the problem they are trying to solve, and the need to solve that problem is more important than producing the correct answer as quickly as possible. In a time when students can search for answers on the internet and high-powered calculators can do the work in an instant, creating these conditions can be a tricky proposition. Milvidskaia explains it using Dan Meyer's (2015) interpretation of Harel's work: "If math is the aspirin, then how do you create the headache? So, if the quadratic formula is the aspirin, what headache was a mathematician trying to solve?" (p. 1). In explaining the idea of students having an intellectual need for the quadratic formula, Milvidskaia shared this example:

> Imagine you had come in and I said, "Hey, Jennifer, I'm thinking of a triangle. It's in my head, and you can ask me for three clues. You can ask me what's the measure of angle blank, or what's the measure of side blank. What are you going to ask me to figure out my triangle?"
>
> So now it's a game, right? What I'm trying to get you to understand is that... in mathematics... there are certain truths. If you ask me about two angles and a side, and that side is between the two angles, you can guarantee the triangle that is in my head. To me that is absolutely beautiful, because you don't need all six pieces of information. You don't need all three angles and all three sides to figure out the triangle in my head.... Mathematically,

what I'm trying to get you to realize are these [ancient] Euclidean principles about how do I prove two triangles are congruent.

But if you instead had come to class and I said, "Today we're going to learn how to prove two triangles are congruent. You need three pieces of information." Many students would be sitting there going, "Why do I need three? Who said three? Why is it not four. Why is it not two?" Right? Cause [if] I was a kid, I would be, like, this is stupid. (personal communication, November 30, 2023)

This example illustrates how teachers can take concepts such as angles and sides and give students a reason to want to understand, to go beyond the need to figure out the answer and also know why it is true. For me as a teacher, memorable moments were those when I was able to spark that curiosity in students to want to dig in, to really want to understand the connections, and to see the need beyond the classroom for the skill or topic we were studying.

Things to Keep in Mind

- **Use the qualitative data you collect.** Qualitative data should help form the basis of the examples you use to make real-world connections for your students. Thinking back to Chapter 2, if you learn on a survey or in a focus group that many students are interested in traveling or sports or cooking, you can use those interests as starting points for making authentic connections. You will also learn which things students find hard to understand or haven't liked over the years. These are opportunities for building that intellectual curiosity and helping students understand why a particular skill or subject is necessary.
- **Have students share their own connections.** The best way to have students see real-world applications of their

learning is to have them share their own connections. Such sharing can happen in a variety of ways. For example, once a week you could have students reflect in writing, in pairs or as a group, on how they used what they were learning in class outside school. This activity gives students the opportunity to hear from one another and review what was covered in class. You could also designate a classroom space where students share examples (through pictures, artifacts, or in writing) of times when they saw what they learned in their daily lives. Such a space can serve as a way for students to review concepts and to learn from one another, and for you to learn more about students' lives.

- **Value your students' process and progress.** Understanding the process that students go through to get to their answer can often tell you more than a right or wrong response will. Focusing on intellectual necessity and helping students to understand the *why* behind what they are doing builds their sense of relevancy and engagement, while supporting learning.

Giving Students Choice

Giving students choice is not a new concept, but it is one that can make a huge impact on how students perceive meaning in their work. Authentic choice is about more than just allowing students to decide if they want to do the even- or odd-numbered problems on a homework assignment; instead, it is about giving them real power over their learning. Students need to feel that they have autonomy over certain decisions, that they can succeed at the task they are being asked to do, and that what they are doing is valuable for their learning and their community.

The following example comes from a former student reflecting on an experience in which she experienced all three of these concepts—autonomy, success, and value—as she worked on a project with her middle school librarian. The project was built around a writing contest based on the book *Wonder*, by R. J. Palacio, which was a schoolwide reading assignment. The autonomy was evident because not only did she choose to do this project on her own time, but it also aligned with her values, her interests, and her goals. She felt appropriately challenged, competent, and validated by her success in completing the project. The value came not only from creating something that could affect every student in the school but also from the sense of belonging she felt with both the staff member she was working with and the students who participated in the writing contest. Here is her account of the experience:

> I had come up with the idea to do a *Wonder* writing contest and have people write their own chapter from another character's point of view that wasn't in the book already. The librarian worked with me during my lunch and after school for about a week helping me create the guidelines for the contest and flyers to send out to the different homerooms. This made me feel extremely validated as a student, especially considering that a faculty member in the school who wasn't even my teacher would put all of this time and energy into helping me bring a project idea to life!

Giving students choice can be a useful strategy when a topic is so broad or complex that you may not have the opportunity to dig into it as much as you would like. For example, when I was teaching about World War II, students were interested in many aspects of what was happening, and we didn't have the time to cover everything together. So after learning about what was happening in general in countries around the world, students could choose something that they wanted to learn more about, do the related research, and present their findings in a format of their choosing. This extension allowed students to start with what they knew, dig deeper into a topic that they were interested in, figure out how that topic affected the outcome of the war, and share their learning with their peers.

Another opportunity for students to exercise choice is through what they are reading. In Chapter 3, we looked at the impact of storytelling on student engagement, which suggests that reading can be a way for students to engage because they see themselves in what they are learning through the stories being highlighted in class. If you use book clubs in your class, you could create a list of books representing a variety of different perspectives on the same topic and let students choose their groups and which book they are going to read from that list. You could also give students a list of novels that fit the standards you are covering and then let them vote on which one they want to read as the class novel. If you have a specific topic that students need to learn more about, have them find relevant articles to share with their classmates. Each of these suggestions helps to change the narrative on whose voice is being featured and what stories are being emphasized.

Giving students choice in how to present their learning is another powerful way to allow them the autonomy they are craving at this age. Whereas some students are content with writing a paper on a topic, others might enjoy more creative ways to share their learning. As long as you have outlined the important pieces to include, giving students the opportunity to choose their mode of presentation can lead to powerful results. Wilfred said she was always looking for creative ways for students to show understanding, including for end-of-unit assessments.

They "could write a narrative from the perspective of the main character and act it out... or... do a dramatic interpretation of one of the scenes and then use evidence as to why they think that the person would recite it in that way... or an interview based on two characters." Wilfred said she was "always thinking what are the ways that you can show understanding that are not just pencil [and] paper? Yes, every student needs to know how to write,... but where are we allowing students to express themselves?" (personal communication, December 8, 2023). Wilfred's question is especially powerful at a time when so many curricula have been scripted and teachers feel that they may not have as many opportunities to be creative in their instruction or to let their students be creative in showing their learning.

Figure 5.1 lists examples of some of the many ways students can share their creativity and learning in any content area that go beyond traditional tests and research papers.

FIGURE 5.1

Creative Ways for Students to Demonstrate Learning

• Cartoon	• Infographic	• PSA/documentary
• Children's book	• Letters	• Skit
• Collage	• Memory box	• Slide presentation
• Commercial	• Model	• Speech
• Diary entries	• Playlist	• Video
• Drawing/painting	• Podcast	
• Essay	• Poetry	

Things to Keep in Mind

- **Start by adding one element of choice in each unit.** Adding an element of choice every day or with every lesson can be overwhelming. Start by adding one area in each unit where students can choose what they are learning or how they share their learning. If you are just starting the practice of choice, this could be as simple as having multiple articles about a topic and allowing students to choose which one they want to read or giving them freedom in choosing who they want to work with on a particular assignment. For assessments, you could offer the option of taking a more traditional assessment, creating a project, or writing a paper. Grading a variety of assessments requires more time, but offering choices allows students to share their learning in a way in which they may feel more confident.

- **Be explicit.** Especially if you give students a choice on a summative assessment, make sure they understand your expectations about what to include and the timeline for completion. Letting them know the requirements up front allows them to make an informed decision about how they can best share their learning. Rubrics with this information can be helpful as students complete a final assessment. In my class, explicit expectations included the following:
  — Number of pages, slides, images, or objects required.
  — Minimum and maximum number of words.
  — Dates for project check-ins, if needed, and the final due date.
  — If a presentation is part of the assignment, a timeframe for how long their live or prerecorded presentation should be.

Learning Relevant Skills

Middle school is a time when students have the opportunity to learn skills that will stay with them for the rest of their life. From sewing in home economics, to learning how to categorize 50 different types of trees based on their leaves, to figuring out how to find relevant sources, many of the people that I talked to mentioned skills they learned in middle school that have stayed with them for many years.

One of my former students recalled an assignment on the endangered tree octopus that included identifying reliable online resources. It not only stuck with her but has now influenced work that she is doing with her own students. "That assignment has stuck with me all these years, and I even... adjusted it to create a lesson plan for my elementary students," she said. Especially in today's media environment, with news coming at us 24/7 from many different sources, understanding how to find reliable sources is a real-world necessity for all students and a skill that can be taught in many different content areas.

Another student's experience reflected the real-world value of debate and competition. She recalled a science competition that taught her not only how to pitch an idea but also how to balance the dynamics of the team members in her group. This idea of students learning through public debate and healthy competition is one that resonates with improvement coach Yekaterina Milvidskaia. Middle school students love to debate with their classmates and their teachers, but only when the experience is authentic. As Milvidskaia states, "There is something really genuine and purposeful in the learning. When you are at this disequilibrium, you have [the students] right where you want them because they need a resolution and they want to understand" (personal communication, November 30, 2023). Her colleague Curtis Taylor added, "As the students are sharing, other students are revising their thinking.... So if you're creating that need and helping them to see these ideas and what holds and what's starting to break when a new idea is presented," then students can get to that resolution they are seeking (personal communication, November 30, 2023). In this type of competition and public debate, with students authentically engaged with their peers, they are able to practice these skills in a real-world setting. The benefits can be significant. In 2023, *Forbes* magazine identified the top 20 skills that employers are looking for in their candidates, including problem solving, communication, and conflict resolution (Tambe, 2023).

In another example, my son shared that his most meaningful experience in middle school was the opportunity to create a podcast with his classmates about a little-known piece of history in our community. With the support of the media specialists at his school, students went on a field trip to the site, learned the history, interviewed relevant people, created a script, and recorded the podcast. In the process, they learned how to work together, ask meaningful questions, and create a compelling story across multiple podcast episodes.

Referring to their work as improvement coaches, Taylor and Milvidskaia shared how they help teachers to intentionally present and call out skills like asking questions, annotating assignments and building on one another's thinking within a task that will help students be successful in math, even if they aren't specifically "math skills." As students begin their task, they are able to see these skills in themselves and recognize it in their peers. Milvidskaia used students' color coding of ideas as one example of how it "might not be obvious to students that they are being mathematical" (personal communication, November 30, 2023). Complimenting a student on their color coding is "not good enough," she said. "You need to go deeper... and explain... why color coding is helping us to be... systematic in the way we're thinking, and why mathematicians value that." The teacher's explanation must be "really concrete... specific... public.... intentional. Middle schoolers are the best BS detectors; it has to be genuine." In this example, students are learning not only about the skill of being systematic, which they need in order to be successful mathematicians, but also how to recognize that skill in themselves and in their peers.

These examples from various subject areas are very different, but they show how connecting to life outside school through translatable skills can make learning more meaningful.

Things to Keep in Mind

- **Help students practice skills in real-world situations.** Giving students the opportunity to practice skills they are learning in meaningful ways helps to keep them engaged. Sometimes such real-world practice involves a certain amount of risk taking. University of Virginia professor Ashlee Sjogren points out that teachers need to think about giving students "opportunities for healthy risk taking" and give them "responsible ways to use their voices to advocate for themselves and their peers in their community" (personal communication, October 20, 2023).
- **Take the time to acknowledge the variety of skills needed to be successful.** Many students have one subject that just comes easier to them than others. They may have no idea why that is the case and why another subject seems equally difficult. The same is true for skills. In the

math example described earlier, we saw how teachers can make learning visible and help students to understand that it takes many different skills to be successful and what might work well for one student (such as color-coding their notes) might not work for another. Pointing out specific skills and acknowledging differing abilities can help students find those skills in themselves or recognize places where they can continue to improve.

Encouraging Interdisciplinary Service Learning

"Find your passion and act on it." That was the motto that hung above my SMART Board as a teacher. I would explain to my students that one thing I wanted to do each year was look for ways to answer the following questions:

- What are you passionate about? If you don't know yet, how can I help you to find that passion?
- What can I do to give you the power and confidence to know you can make a difference?

These questions are similar to the longer list of questions in Chapter 1 that the Search Institute identified for helping students find their spark. For me, interdisciplinary service learning provided a way to help my students answer both of these questions. During my time in the classroom, service learning, or the opportunity for students to learn through meaningful engagement with their community, was my favorite way to help students see the connection between what we were learning in the classroom and their life outside school. In projects grounded in service learning, many of my students really dug into something they were passionate about and wanted to see changed in the world. It was more than just a research project, and for some, it ended up having connections to their future careers. As one of my former students stated, "The most meaningful project I did in middle school was our research project on child abuse. I felt like this began to turn gears in my head towards the type of career work I want to do.... I also feel like it opened up a lot of questions and... was meaningful because it really [made] you look for evidence to back up your ideas."

For this interdisciplinary English language arts (ELA) and social studies project, students conducted research, created a public service announcement (PSA) or short documentary, and took meaningful action on their chosen area of focus. Though the project may seem daunting, given the number of moving parts, it truly was worth the effort. Students learned many relevant skills, including finding reliable sources, effective communication through multiple mediums, planning and preparation over an extended period of time, how to self-evaluate and evaluate others, and the importance of reflection. From the teacher standpoint, it allowed my coworkers and me to be guides and to learn alongside our students. This project gave students the opportunity to make choices, learn relevant skills that they could use in and out of school, and see how they could make a meaningful impact in the world.

To help students find an area of focus, this particular project started with a study of the fight for rights, using novels in ELA and a thematic social studies unit that focused specifically on the fight for equal rights throughout U.S. history. Students learned the many ways different groups fought for their rights, discussed which rights they believed were most important, became more aware of which rights are still being fought for, and investigated the rights they saw being violated both in the United States and around the world. The unit culminated with a study of the

Declaration of Human Rights and students choosing one right to focus on in order to answer these three overarching questions:

- In what ways are basic human rights being infringed?
- How can documentaries and PSAs be useful mediums to evoke change?
- What simple steps can people take to make a difference?

Once students had picked an area of focus, they paired up and began working on the first stage of a six-step process: investigation. This stage was followed by planning and preparation, taking action, reflection, demonstration/celebration, and evaluation.

Investigation

First, students investigated their chosen issue. The investigation involved each student doing their own extensive research of the issue, along with identifying potential solutions and actions they could take. In ELA and social studies, students read about people who had taken action to solve a problem. This enabled the students to better understand what types of action they could take. Once they finished their individual research, the pairs of students used their information to jointly write a one-page summary that included the *who, what, where, when,* and *why* of the issue. This step helped them process the differences in what they had found in their individual research and come to a cohesive understanding of their topic.

Planning and Preparation

At this stage, students planned the learning products and service activities needed for a successful project, including a timeline, a detailed outline of their project, and a one-page letter to administration that included a brief explanation of their topic, what they planned to accomplish, how their project might affect the school day or what resources they needed for after-school activities, and how they planned to accomplish their goal. This stage gave them an authentic audience to share their initial thoughts with, and it enabled them to get feedback on their project from someone other than their classroom teachers or peers.

Taking Action

This stage was the heart of the project and took the most time. Students created their PSA or documentary to be shared widely, and they engaged in meaningful service of their choice to benefit the community. To prepare for creating their PSAs and documentaries, students watched examples and thought about what messages were being conveyed. They used these examples to think about the answers to the following questions for their own messaging:

- What do we want people to know about our area of focus?
- After watching our PSA or documentary, what do we want people to feel about our area of focus?
- What do we want people to think about as they watch our PSA or documentary?
- What do we want people to do, now that they understand the issue better?

They learned about writing scripts, thinking specifically about the following:

- A clear audience and purpose
- Messaging in a memorable way that benefits the community and includes the most essential information first
- A call to action

They also assigned roles for creating their PSA or documentary, including the following:

- Script writers
- On-screen talent
- Directors
- Camera people
- Field talent

Students then put together their plan for taking meaningful action. We gave them a version of the chart shown in Figure 5.2 to help brainstorm ideas. The goal was for them to do at least two of these items, one from Column 1 and one from either Column 2 or Column 3. As you can see, each category includes an element of choice, and we had lists of organizations and people that we were connected to at school or in the community to make this a more seamless process.

Reflection

During this stage, students reflected about how their project was going and what they learned from the work. Each time they worked on their project, they completed a reflection using a form such as the one in Figure 5.3. This reflection allowed all teachers involved in the project to be able to support students regardless of which class they were in at the time.

Demonstration/Celebration

During the demonstration/celebration stage, students publicly shared what they had learned, celebrated the results of their actions, and looked to the future. Students began by sharing their work to their individual class before doing so on a public website, during morning announcements, and sometimes at a

FIGURE 5.2
Chart for Brainstorming Ideas to Take Action

Column 1: Raise Awareness	Column 2: Advocate	Column 3: Participate
Create a flyer or fact sheet that helps share information about your cause or an event you want to promote.	Write a newspaper editorial or a letter to a government official. Share what you have learned and your call to action.	Volunteer for an organization that supports the cause you researched.
Create a set of social media posts and a hashtag for your campaign to share on the school's social media sites.	Create a petition that communicates your goal and gather signatures to support the change.	Plan an event that gets others involved in your cause.
Your choice! What's another way you could put together information to raise awareness for your intended audience?	Your choice! What's another way you can advocate for your cause?	Your choice! What's another meaningful way for you to share your time and talent to support your cause?

FIGURE 5.3
Reflection Form for Student Projects

Date	How is your project going?	What questions do you have? What can I (as the teacher) help you with?	What is one thing you learned today?
	1—Struggling 2—Catching up 3—On track 4—Ahead of schedule		

"red carpet event" on the big screen at a local theater. An authentic audience gave students the opportunity to gather feedback and see the impact of their work in real time.

Evaluation

After the demonstration/celebration stage, students evaluated their learning both as an individual and for their peers. Often in these types of projects, the process and the learning are even more important than the final product. The students used the same rubric that we did as teachers, looking for the following elements:

- Content that was relevant and detailed
  - A clearly stated cause
  - A well-defined call to action
- Visuals, narration, and sound that were relevant, intriguing, and kept the audience's attention
  - Photos
  - Videos with an expert interviewee
  - Voiceovers/narration
  - Music/sound effects
  - Transitions

Sometimes this type of project continues to grow in unexpected ways. If that happens, it is important for teachers to evaluate their capacity to support students over the longer term, and students must evaluate their commitment to the cause. In my case, as you will read about in Chapter 7, what started as letters to our congresswoman about the importance of ending child labor around the world led to a multiyear opportunity for students to learn about fundraising, marketing, outreach, event planning, and making an impact through music, community events, and advocacy with their elected officials. This reflection from a former student, now an educator herself, shows how important this kind of learning is:

> The most meaningful part of middle school was realizing how much of an impact I could make at such a young age. I was able to organize events and raise funds for A Better Life for Kids during my time in middle school with the help and support of amazing peers and teachers who shared a vision. I learned how to work together with others and collaborate during these experiences. I learned that my voice mattered. The walk-a-thon at the end of my 8th-grade year was a great way to celebrate the hard work and collaboration from the year. The teachers that I had in middle school made a lasting impact on my life and helped me develop passions that I have today.

Things to Keep in Mind

- **Don't try to do everything at once.** The project as described took multiple months for students to complete, went through a couple of different iterations over the years, and required a team of teachers working closely together to make it successful. Through trial and error, we were able to craft a timeline that allowed for the infusion of content and service learning. We also made sure that we were meeting standards for social studies, ELA, and social-emotional learning. If you want to try something like this, start small with one aspect of the project and continue to build from there.

  Starting small could mean having students pick a topic, investigate it, and then put together a presentation to share with a larger audience. Gradually scaling, you could then add having students use their voice to raise awareness, advocate, or participate using examples like the ones described earlier. From there, you could then add even more ways for students to take meaningful action or add an authentic audience for them to share their learning with before moving to a project at the scale described in this chapter.

- **Encourage students to talk to experts.** In their research and in their advocacy, encourage students to find local organizations and people doing the work and then to interview them or to ask about volunteer opportunities. Doing so allows students to feel a connection to the work being done and to gather expert voices to make their story and advocacy even more compelling.
- **Have students present to an authentic audience.** If students are engaged in learning that affects their community, give them the opportunity to present and get feedback from that community. This could take the form of sharing their work with leaders of nonprofits doing similar work or government officials from the community that has been affected. These leaders can help students understand if their project is feasible and would have the intended impact. Students could also gather feedback from the people who were directly affected by the project.
- **Serve as a guide.** This type of project requires teachers to share power with students and let them take the lead in their learning. Sharing power is one of the elements of the Developmental Relationships Framework developed by the Search Institute (2020), and it is often one of the most challenging for teachers to embrace. Sharing power means that your job is to give guidelines and support and to let the students lead as much as possible. Doing so can feel uncomfortable at first, but it leads to students feeling

empowered and that they have an authentic say in their learning. This point leads to my next piece of advice.
- **Be OK with the unknown!** Sometimes an experience like this one can take you and your students to a place you had not anticipated. Embrace the experience and enjoy the ride!

Wrapping It Up

Though every moment of every school day isn't going to capture a student's attention, it is important for students to understand the *why* behind what they are learning. As educators, this means that we have created an environment where students see the necessity of understanding the material that is presented. This environment can come in the form of small opportunities for students to make connections to their daily life or larger opportunities that allow them to explore something they are passionate about and share that learning with others. Use the questions in Figure 5.4 to get started on connecting learning to life outside school as a way to spark student interest.

FIGURE 5.4
Finding the SPARK for Connecting Learning to Life Outside School

Study—What data do you already have about what students are interested in or where they are struggling? What data might you want to collect related to your content area?

Pilot—What are easy opportunities to infuse students' experiences outside the classroom into your curriculum?

Analyze—What data can you collect and analyze that helps you understand the impact on your classroom community when students have the opportunity to see their life outside school reflected in the classroom?

Reflect—How did it feel to make connections to students' lived experiences? For you? For your students?

Kindle—Are you ready to do more? What other opportunities are there in your curriculum or your community to add these types of connections?

6

Finding the Spark Every Day

> *Sparks are the hidden flames in your*
> *kids that light their proverbial fire,*
> *get them excited, tap into their true passions.*
>
> —Peter L. Benson, *Sparks: How Parents Can Help*
> *Ignite the Hidden Strengths of Teenagers*

It's a Friday in April, right at the beginning of the fourth quarter in 7th grade. Students are walking in feeling excited because it's finally warming up and staying light past 7 p.m., which is a welcome change after the cold darkness of a Chicago winter. On Thursday, students had completed a quick reflection survey about the third quarter, and overnight I had analyzed the results and had some questions for my class around areas of support and next steps. On the board is a graph that shows how many students felt they got the support they needed to be successful in class during the third quarter. The chart skews positive, with 68 percent of students answering "agree" or "strongly agree," but as a teacher I'm concerned that just over 30 percent didn't feel that way (especially since that number is up from 20 percent after the second quarter).

There are two reflection questions on the board: *What does support look like to you? How can I support you better in this class?* I make sure students know that their answers can be anonymous if they prefer, but if there's something specific they want me to know or do for them, then a name is helpful. Students get started right away, and within a few minutes I have a ton of additional information about what support looks like to them and how I can better meet their needs for the last quarter of the year. Because students feel their voice is being heard and we often look at data this way, students share honestly, knowing that I will take their thoughts seriously and make changes to better support their learning.

Throughout this book, I have shared big and small ways to ignite the spark in young people's learning and engagement. Though the chapters are separated by the themes of adolescent development, reflecting on data, storytelling, integrating art, and connecting learning to life outside school, many of these themes overlap. This chapter focuses on simple ways to infuse this type of learning into your classroom daily, along with activities that highlight the overlaps between these different themes.

Creating Daily "Sparks" of Connection

Helping students to connect to their learning, to create those sparks that Benson refers to, can't be a once-a-month or once-a-quarter thing. As a teacher, take at least five minutes every day to plan how to help students create those meaningful connections. Whether it's through storytelling, the arts, or tying a topic to something in their life outside school, the sense making that comes from those intentional activities will help students to remember what they learned, connect it to other learning, and see ways to integrate it into their lives.

One way to be intentional about this "spark time" is to create weekly themes or a monthly calendar to make the effort visible to students. For each of these ideas, students can share their thoughts in pairs or small groups, through a collective or individual written response, or as a whole class. For example, a weekly calendar could include days of the week that focus on a different theme:

- **Meaningful Monday:** Have students share one thing that they learned the week before or in the unit you are currently studying that they used outside school.
- **Talented Tuesday:** Have students connect a form of art to the content you are learning. This could be a piece of art that they find or something that you have them react to or create.
- **Why Wednesday:** Give students a dedicated opportunity to ask questions about what they are learning. The questions could be about things they find confusing, places where they need additional information, or the ever-present "Why are we learning this?" question. Some students can be apprehensive about asking for help, so giving them the opportunity to do this every week can make the practice more routine and help all students to advocate for what they need.
- **Talkative Thursday:** Have students share a story about themselves related to the content they are learning or something that is happening in the school.
- **Facts and Figures Friday:** Share data from the week with your students in order to gather additional feedback from them on one or more aspects of your class. Like the example that opens this chapter, these data could come from a more formal survey regarding classroom culture. But it

also could be looking at one question that many students missed on an assessment or an assignment that many students didn't turn in to find out why. As discussed in Chapter 2, make sure this is information that you are ready to hear and that you do this in such a way that the students feel that their voice will be valued and that their thoughts and opinions will be heard and acted upon.

If monthly themes fit better into your planning, here are examples of specific focuses for each month:

- **Storytelling September:** To build connections to start the year, use this month to have students share their own stories in a variety of ways, using ideas from Chapter 3.
- **Options and Opportunities October:** Giving options and new opportunities to your students could be as simple as letting them choose which question they answer as an opener or other ideas from Chapter 5. Having students making choices about what works best for them gives them more confidence and allows them to see that their opinions have value.
- **Noticings November:** Take time each day to gather observations, opinions, and ideas from students. These might be about how their first months of school have gone or what they thought of a particular assignment or project. Soliciting your students' voices early and often will give them practice in sharing their thoughts and feelings throughout the year. In Chapter 2, there are many options for ways to gather street-level data from your students.
- **Data Dive December:** As the first semester comes to an end, use this month to share data with students and gather additional feedback from them to make changes for the

second semester. Chapter 2 has ideas for ways to gather feedback and use data to co-create with your students.

- **Journaling January:** The beginning of the calendar year is always a good time to reflect on the year that has just ended and set goals for the new year. Throughout January, give students the opportunity to engage in a dialogue journal with you (see Chapter 3) or reflect on goals they set for themselves. Second semester in any grade in middle school often sees big changes, especially as 6th graders are getting comfortable with being middle schoolers, 7th graders are thinking about what it will mean to be the oldest students in the building in just a few short months, and 8th graders are thinking about high school. Journaling can give students the opportunity to share their thoughts, and it allows teachers to gain insights into how their students are feeling.
- **Flair February:** February can be a tough month at school. It can be cold and dreary, depending on your location, or maybe it's just the time of year that seems to drag. Use this month to brighten up your curriculum by intentionally sharing art that connects to the students' learning each day. The "flair" that comes from visual art, music, cartoons, photographs, and other forms can revitalize this time of year and give students landmarks to connect their learning to. Chapter 4 offers many examples of ways to bring the arts into your classroom.
- **March Madness:** Playing off the annual basketball tournament, create a bracket of various activities for students to do each day that connect to your curriculum. An example of this could be a storytelling activity versus an art activity, or a drawing activity versus a music activity.

Throughout the month, have students choose (and do!) the activity, while voting along the way to get to a final winning activity that students connected to the most. This activity allows you to revisit themes from the past months and see what really stuck with students or what they found most engaging throughout the year.

- **Advice April:** Throughout the month, have students do a series of reflection activities, beginning with the advice they would give to students coming into the grade or class. Then have them think about things that they wish they had known before starting the year. Find ways to share the insights with incoming students, whether through short videos or writing or even presenting to their younger peers, if possible. These activities can be beneficial for both you as the teacher and for your current and future students. They give students the opportunity to reflect on how they have grown throughout the year, what changes they have made, and points at which they wish they had done something differently. For you as the teacher, hearing this advice can help you to think differently about how to welcome students into your classroom, or it can help you to consider small changes that can help students be more successful.
- **Making Meaning May:** As the year comes to an end, May is a good time to review everything students have learned during the year, have them create a through line between the different units, and think about how the skills and topics they learned about in all of their classes connect to one another. This thematic focus helps to build relevancy and student understanding of the interconnectedness of the various elements of their learning.

Things to Keep in Mind

- **Be flexible but consistent.** Things will always come up during a school year that will make you feel like you never have enough time—the assembly that gets added at the last minute, the fire drill that knocks 10 minutes off your class period, or the testing schedule that keeps you from seeing half your students for a number of days. These are all things that come up regularly for educators everywhere. Even with disruptions, it's important to stay as consistent as possible. If you try the weekly schedule described earlier but need to skip a day or move a topic, let students know why. If you try a monthly theme, make sure to do enough activities throughout the month for students to connect to the theme.
- **Let others know what you are doing.** It's always easier to continue a new initiative when you know you have support. Teaching can sometimes feel incredibly lonely. Though you are constantly surrounded by people, the four walls of your classroom can sometimes feel very confining. Remember, though, that there are many people who want you to succeed, and letting others know what you are doing can help to both keep you accountable and to inspire others to do the same. Sometimes finding the spark for a teacher is just as important as finding it for students.

Overlapping Themes

As I reflected on everything that I had heard from students, researchers, educators, and analysts while writing this book, I saw distinctions in how the themes of storytelling, integration of art, and connecting learning to the outside world created sparks of engagement for students, but I also noticed links that can be helpful in meeting the unique needs of middle schoolers. Knowing how hard it can be to try multiple new ideas, given all the expectations put on educators, in the next sections of this chapter I show how these themes—along with the points made in earlier chapters about student data and adolescent brain development—can be combined and integrated into your curriculum.

Student Data + Storytelling + Connections to Life Outside School

As educators, we gather a lot of data from students every day through assignments, informal observations, and short written or verbal check-ins. Intentionality in both collecting and organizing the data to better understand the story it tells allows you to make informed decisions about how to best support student learning and growth. Before collecting any type of data, ask yourself the following questions:

- What am I hoping to learn from this piece of data?
- How will I use this data to offer feedback or support to my students?
- How am I hoping this data will inform my next steps?

Once you have reflected on the reasons behind collecting the data, you can begin to use the information more effectively to understand how students are experiencing your classroom and interacting with the material. Check-in questions and learning connections are two ways to gain this understanding.

Check-In Questions

In Chapter 3, we looked at the idea of asking a Question of the Day. Though similar, check-in questions are really about gathering information about how students are feeling or how they understood something that you taught in class. They can be used for a variety of purposes, including as a social-emotional check-in, a way to spark connection to a topic that students will be learning about, or a way to elicit storytelling to strengthen your classroom community. These types of questions can also help you to clear up misconceptions about a concept, understand what students already know about a topic, get a general sense of students' mood, or learn more about their lives in and outside the classroom.

Here are some ideas for check-in questions and prompts:

- **Explain how you are feeling, using _____ (weather, animals, emojis, food, etc.).** Have students share what they are feeling in terms of a category (for weather, that could be sunny, partly sunny, stormy, gray skies, tornado, hurricane). You could have them explain why they are feeling a particular way, or you could just get a general mood check of your class based on how many "sunny" versus "stormy" answers you get. If you do this activity regularly, you can also track the moods of individual students to better support those who regularly identify as having more perceived negative emotions.
- **Share one thing that comes to mind when you think about _____.** The fill-in-the-blank content could be something you are getting ready to study, something you've already studied, or something that is happening at the school. You could have students write their answers on sticky notes or share with a partner and then out loud with the class. This activity allows you to gather additional data on the themes across answers and support students if they have questions or misconceptions.

- **What's a _____ (rose/thorn, peak/valley, positive/ negative, learning/understanding, sun/cloud) for this week?** Giving students time to share their positives and negatives from the week can both facilitate storytelling and give you additional data on how students are experiencing their school day. You can confine the experiences to those related to just your class or their school day, or expand it to activities outside school, depending on your answer to the question of why you are collecting this information.

Connections

Chapter 5 focused on the importance of connecting learning to students' lives. Having students share those connections daily can help you to understand what they are taking from your lesson and how they engaged with the material you presented. One idea for how to do this is having students engage in a sentence-stem activity in which students share their answers to the following questions:

- The most interesting thing I learned in class today was _____.
- I can connect what I learned today to _____.
- I want to share what I learned today with _____ because _____.
- One question I have is _____.

The data you collect from this type of activity gives you valuable insights into not only the questions that students have about the material but also their immediate thoughts on what they can do with this information.

Storytelling + Identity Formation

In Chapter 1, we looked at the importance of identity formation and students having the opportunity to figure out who they are in relation to their school community and the world outside the school. One important aspect of that identity formation comes from students being able to share their own stories and to hear from others about experiences that are similar and different from their own. Two ways to infuse that kind of storytelling into the classroom are by finding sources that present multiple perspectives on an issue or event and giving students opportunities to share their own stories.

Stories from Multiple Perspectives

If your class is learning about a specific time period or event, find short, first-person accounts of the event from multiple perspectives. These could be quotes or short articles or even letters or diary entries. Another option is to use children's books written about the topic. Have groups of students read the different accounts, looking for similarities and differences in how the story is told and how the event affected each person or group of people. Students can then reflect on how reading these differing experiences can help give a more complete understanding of what happened.

Students Sharing Their Stories

In Chapter 3, we looked at ways for students to share stories about their family history, but another option is to take a few minutes a couple of times a week to have students share their own personal story to build community and connection. Give students a basic template of ideas to choose from, such as the following:

- How they got their name
- What they like to do for fun outside school
- What their favorites are (food, color, animal, sport, book, song, subject)
- What their strengths are (especially for the class that they are in)
- Who is in their family
- An interesting fact they want to share
- A quote that inspires them
- A picture of their favorite place to visit or a place they want to visit

Tell students that they will have three to five minutes to share as much as they want about themselves with their classmates. During the first few weeks of school, have one or two students a day share their story. Make sure to model this activity with your own story, and provide as much scaffolding as you think your students may need.

Arts Integration + Understanding Emotions

In Chapter 4, we looked at many ways to infuse various art forms into classroom learning. Giving students art-based landmarks to connect to their learning can help them remember what they learned and put their learning into the larger context of the unit or lesson. Art can also help students better understand and express emotions, especially as they are grappling with who they are, who they want to be, and what that means for their friendships, academics, and how they spend their time outside school.

Students often engage in a kind of informal art creation, such as folding paper to make animal shapes or doodling on their notes, on their tests, or on any surface available. It always made me happy to see the pictures students randomly drew to illustrate a concept in the margins of a page or on a note of appreciation or even a note expressing confusion about an assignment. I also found folded-paper roses, cranes, or frogs left by students to decorate my desk. Instead of seeing this kind of informal art merely as something whimsical that students do on their own, see it as something you can use to your advantage. For example, as students come into class, have them draw something that does one of the following:

- Expresses how they are feeling that day
- Shows their level of understanding about a topic
- Answers a prompt that is written on the board

Brooklyn Raney (personal communication, February 2, 2024) shared an activity that she calls "messy mural," in which students draw or write on a giant piece of paper to express their reaction to a prompt. The students are all drawing or writing at the same time, on different parts of the paper, and they shift positions as new prompts are given. The result is a messy and somewhat chaotic mural. Because everyone is drawing or writing at once, there is less pressure around being "right" or the best artist. This engaging and memorable activity can give teachers a lot of information about what their students know, understand, and feel about a topic. Raney does something similar with torn paper, having students tear a small piece of paper into a shape to respond to a prompt. For example, the teacher could ask students to tear the paper into their favorite animal or a food that they would like to try. Though the paper may not look anything like what they were trying to convey, the simple act of tearing the paper and explaining the shape to someone else brings that art connection (and a little bit of laughter and fun) into the classroom.

Connecting Life Outside School + Finding the *Why*

Finding out the *why* behind something is an important pursuit for middle school students. They might be trying to determine the *why* for a lesson or the *why* behind something their friend did; perhaps they want to know *why* a system is functioning in a certain way. Helping middle schoolers find answers to these questions is essential, and two ways to do so are through a share-out activity and by tapping into the expertise of people with relevant experience.

The Share-Out

Sometimes understanding the *why* can be achieved through something as simple as a share-out by students. If students seem to be struggling to understand a concept or how it could apply outside the classroom, stop the lesson for a few minutes to gain some insights. Acknowledge that you see a lot of confused expressions or a lack of students participating in the discussion. Ask your students if they are noticing the same thing or feeling the same way. From there, ask if there are any students who can share ways that they have seen the concept you are discussing play out in their world or if they can help other students make connections in that moment. As mentioned earlier in this chapter, you can also create intentional space each week for students to share ways they have used their learning outside the classroom. Depending on the topic, you could record these share-outs and add to them throughout the unit. For some units, I even had a dedicated space in the classroom where students could add sample artifacts related to places or situations where they were able to make a connection to what we learned in class.

Finding an Expert

The staff in any building is made up of a diverse group of people with a variety of backgrounds. Tapping into their experiences can help make curriculum come alive for students and help them to see how what they are learning is relevant to their life outside school. When I was teaching about catalogs and how mail order changed access to manufactured products for people in rural areas, I invited one of my friends who had lived on a farm during her childhood to come and share that experience with my students. She talked about getting the catalog and circling the things she wanted, and then having the order arrive by train. Her presentation not only helped students to understand what a big change this was but also to hear about it from someone who had experienced it firsthand. Tapping into the experience and expertise of your colleagues and others can really help students see the real-world effects of things they are learning about in the classroom.

Things to Keep in Mind

- **Play to your strengths (at first).** Some people excel in storytelling, and others, in music. Some people can easily explain the connections between what they are teaching and how it affects life outside school, while others love thinking about how to effectively use data. Start with your strength in building connections for and with students. After you effectively incorporate one of these practices in your teaching, then you can add more throughout the year, building your own comfort level and confidence while finding new ways to engage your students.
- **Use the ideas in this book to ignite your own spark!** Doing something new not only will engage your students

but also can be a great way to reignite your own creativity. You never know what will land with students until you try. Hopefully some of the ideas in this book will give you a new outlook on your students, your curriculum, and ways to engage with the broader community.

Wrapping It Up

Renowned educator and school reform advocate Marva Collins once said, "Once children learn how to learn, nothing is going to narrow their mind. The essence of teaching is to make learning contagious, to have one idea spark another" (Collins & Tamarkin, 1990, p. 147).

Prioritizing time each day for creating sparks and connections, whether to another student, to a teacher, or to the curriculum, is always time well spent. These connections are where meaning is made for students as they have experiences, take in information, and process it. On the other side of that meaning making is the learning and development we are all striving for.

Use the questions in the chart in Figure 6.1 to make finding the spark an everyday experience.

FIGURE 6.1
Finding the SPARK Every Day

Study—Where do you see overlaps in the ideas shared in this book?

Pilot—What ideas could you combine in your classroom to create a more meaningful experience for students?

Analyze—What engagement data would you want to collect to see if what you implemented is working?

Reflect—Where do you see student engagement happening in your classroom already? How can you build on that?

Kindle—How do you keep your own spark going?

7

The Path Forward

Hope is a discipline.... It's work to be hopeful. It's not like a fuzzy feeling.... You have to actually put in energy, time, and you have to be clear-eyed, and you have to hold fast to having a vision. It's a hard thing to maintain. But it matters to have it, to believe that it's possible, to change the world.

—Mariame Kaba, activist and educator

The path through adolescence is often portrayed as a straight line. Students go from 6th grade to 7th grade to 8th grade and then on to high school. It seems so straightforward, yet what it ends up looking like is a jumbled maze of emotions, experiences, and changes with a lot of learning along the way.

I spent most of my career teaching 7th grade, but every so often I would have the opportunity to teach a section or two of 6th or 8th grade. It was always eye-opening to see the stark differences between these three grades—physically, academically, and socially. Sixth graders are learning how to open a combination locker, figuring out how to get to class on time, and checking

Google Classroom for assignments, all while navigating multiple classes with multiple teachers and different combinations of students. Even if schools have good systems in place to welcome students, this transition can still be overwhelming for so many. In 7th grade, students are definitely more comfortable in the school but are often less comfortable in their own bodies. As discussed in Chapter 1, this is a time when so many changes are happening, and students are working to figure out who they are and who they want to be. In 7th grade, I would see students start the year shorter than my own five-foot-three-inch self and end the year a full head taller. Voices would become deeper, and the shape of bodies would change. Friendships would come and go, sometimes disrupting relationships that students had had since kindergarten. By 8th grade, students would start their year feeling surer of themselves and more confident in their abilities. Many would step into leadership roles not just in classes but also on sports teams, after-school clubs, and student council. But as the year went on, some students would begin to show fear about the unknowns of high school, causing them to act out or slip into the background, while others couldn't wait to get out to see what was next.

As educators, we have the opportunity to help shape this path in so many ways. Take a few minutes to reflect on the following questions:

- What do you remember most about your own middle school experience? Do you have more positive or negative memories?
- Is there a project or experience that you remember most? Or a teacher? A friend?
- What do you hope your students say about their middle school experience?

- What skills, experiences, and opportunities do you want them to have?
- How does your school already support these ideas? What would need to change to make these goals a reality?

As you read the following story, think about which elements of your own middle school memory or hopes for your own students are highlighted.

Finding a Path

In thinking about the questions just presented in terms of my own classroom and students, I reflect on an experience about 10 years into my teaching career that ended up including all of the themes in this book but started with a simple assignment.

In the fall of 2009, I returned to the classroom about seven months after welcoming my second child. By that winter of 2010, I was finally getting into the groove of what it meant to be a working parent with two kids. In my social studies classes, we had just finished learning about the rights children have around the world and where those rights were being violated. On a day I was out for a conference, I had my classes write letters to their elected officials—Congresswoman Jan Schakowsky, Senator Dick Durbin, and President Barack Obama—to voice their opinions on the UN Convention on the Rights of the Child and to speak up for children who are forced to work in often dangerous conditions to help support themselves and their families. I also had them share, based on what they had learned in class, what they felt should be done about the system worldwide. When I returned the following day and saw what they had written, I was inspired by their commitment to the cause and the powerful words they had spoken based on their own stories, experiences, and understandings of the issue. As I wrestled with the copier to make three copies of each of the 125 letters and then bundled them up to be sent to each individual elected official, I remember assuming that we wouldn't get a response but still feeling hopeful as I knew my students had made compelling arguments that deserved to be heard.

About a month later, after arriving at school early in the morning, I opened my school email inbox and saw an email address that I didn't recognize but that had a "mail.house.gov" ending. As I opened the message, I realized that it actually was from Congresswoman Schakowsky's office, and it said not only that she had received the letters but also that she wanted to come and speak with the 7th graders who had written them. I couldn't believe it! After quickly checking with our principal about the feasibility of this request and getting his enthusiastic approval, I immediately sent a response to better understand the logistics and set up the visit. Surprisingly, we were quickly able to agree on a date and time, and then I was able to share the exciting news with my students. In class, we prepped for her visit by thinking through questions to ask and learning more about the work she had already done on this issue in Congress. Like the students, I was nervous and excited in anticipation of the event.

On the day of Congresswoman Schakowsky's visit, all 125 7th graders and my fellow teachers gathered in the multipurpose room to hear her speak. In her speech, the congresswoman shared many things, but the sentiment that stuck out to me the most was the idea that writing letters is great, but, as she told the students, if you really want to make an impact, you have to do more. You must get the message out to the world and inspire people to take real action.

The next day, as we reflected on her visit, I repeated that sentiment to each of my classes. I told them I was proud of them for taking the first step and to know that their voice had been heard. I also told them that if they wanted to stop there, we could, but if they wanted to do more, then I was there to support them; however, they needed to take the lead. The students in the first couple of classes said they wanted to think about it, but in one of my afternoon classes, a student who struggled and was often off task raised his hand. He looked very serious as he asked if we could potentially do a walk-a-thon during the school day to raise both awareness in the community and potentially money for an organization that supported children's rights. I remember, as his classmates praised his idea, being so excited to see him shine and thrive in that moment. After I got permission for the walk-a-thon from my principal, this student began to take the lead in a way I had never seen before. He helped with logistics, the subsequent T-shirt design contest, and the actual event at the end of the year. Because of his idea and his leadership thereafter, a new club was formed that continued to exist long past his time at the school. Hundreds of students and community members participated in an annual walk-a-thon and other fundraising activities, and thousands of dollars were raised to support children worldwide.

From that moment on, in my class and in many others, that student and others who joined him in the effort found their voice and understood that they could make an impact. Using compelling storytelling, they shared their own story and the stories of children they had never met, many living in places thousands of miles away, as a way to inspire people toward action. Using art, they shared the goal of their work on T-shirts, posters, and later on cups, notepads, and even lunchbox sandwich cases. They also made commercials to advertise and share additional information. All of this was part of a real-world experience that allowed students to bring about real change. And since then, some of those same students have gone on to join similar efforts in high school or college, some have run for office, and some have pursued other careers that fulfill their desire to make an impact on the world.

I realized through that experience that my hope for all students is to know that they have the ability to make a difference. I want all students to be able to live out the mantra that hung in my classroom and be able to find their passion and take action. Though not every student will have the specific walk-a-thon opportunity I have described, every student should have a school experience that makes them feel that their voice is heard and valued by their community.

A Changing World

A lot has changed in our world and in education since that walk-a-thon experience in 2010. Education encompasses so many different types of communities, schools, educators, and students. As I interviewed educators, researchers, students, coaches, and data strategists from across the United States, I asked each of them what they felt had changed the most in the post-pandemic environment and what they were most excited and nervous about when it comes to education. The answers were varied but ultimately centered around some important themes.

First, there were positive changes, such as students being more willing to share and be honest about their experiences in school. People talked about how students are asking more challenging questions and using their voice as leaders to insist on something better for themselves and their peers. Others mentioned that their students have a collective sense of humor and are lifting each other up and are willing to help one another in ways that weren't as evident before 2020.

On the concerning front, there were worries about larger influences such as polarization and attacks on public schools and what that will mean for teacher retention and for the institution that is meant to provide a collective experience and understanding for our society. There was concern about the hopelessness that comes with growing up in a seemingly dysfunctional world. Some educators mentioned that they have noticed an apathy around homework, a yearning for socialization but a struggle to engage in group work, and some students shutting down at the first roadblock they encounter. They also expressed concern over students who say that they aren't interested in anything and don't seem to have that spark that fosters a connection to school or to their future.

But these conversations also revealed many reasons for hope. People talked about the renewed focus on mental health and social-emotional learning and the need to center relationships and connections. They mentioned wanting to help students be adaptable and flexible in a world that is moving quickly and always changing, along with wanting students to have more opportunities to learn things they are interested in learning about and to continue their education. People saw a need for more media literacy and understanding the news beyond the headlines, along with a focus on critical-thinking skills, especially with changes due to artificial intelligence and the very real worry about addiction to technology. People also mentioned wanting to provide safety, connectedness, and purpose, along with making sure that educational resources are allocated equitably.

So What's Next?

As I listened to all these different people talk about their experiences and thought back on my own experiences with students, I found myself reflecting on the power of education and how much it influences all parts of society. I was inspired by the many individuals who are thinking about the ways they were affected by their time in middle school and their ideas for either improving on or replicating those experiences for young people today. I left the conversations hopeful after hearing about the ways that educators continue to find opportunities to instill a sense of purpose and relevancy into their daily practices. In *Portrait of a Thriving Youth* (Youth-Nex, 2023), the authors explain that developing a sense of meaning and purpose in adolescence can be a key force for young people to continue moving forward with positivity and feel a sense of worth and value.

The preceding chapters have provided examples for how to help students develop that sense of meaning and purpose through storytelling, art, and connecting learning to life outside school by recognizing where students are developmentally, listening to what they have to say about their experiences, and co-creating changes and new experiences alongside them. This multifaceted task may sound like a lot, and it certainly can be. Implementing significant changes in the classroom can be hard, especially on top of all the other things that teachers are asked to do. With that in mind, here are some suggestions and questions to help you get started:

- Begin with what you know.
  - Which chapter in this book resonated with you the most?

- Which chapter (storytelling, integrating art, or connections to life outside the classroom) best fits into your current curriculum?
- What is one activity you could try tomorrow?
- Revamp and improve.
  - When you read about a specific idea or project, did one of your existing units or lessons come to mind that you are now thinking about in a different way?
  - What is something that you read that could be incorporated into that existing unit or lesson?
- Build for the future.
  - Is there a unit or lesson that you know you want to change or stop using because it hasn't been working for your students?
  - Is there an idea or experience that you want to add because of something that you read?
  - What information would you need to gather from students to better meet their needs?
- Dream big.
  - What does your ideal school look like?
  - What dreams do you have for yourself?
  - What dreams do you have for your students?
  - What does it mean to you to see a spark of learning in your students?

Once you have answered these questions for yourself, and if you have decided to make a larger change that requires the involvement of other people, begin to build buy-in. Think about the following things:

- Presenting your idea
  - Who needs to know about your new idea?

- What venues are available for you to present the idea (e.g., grade-level team meeting, content team meeting, all-staff meeting, open house, email communication, survey)?
- What type of feedback are you hoping to receive after presenting your idea?
- What will you do with that feedback?
• Collaborating with others
    - How could collaboration make your new idea even stronger?
    - Who could you collaborate with to bring this new idea to life?
    - Who would be your biggest supporter in making this new idea a success?
• Getting approval and support
    - Do you need to get approval to implement your idea?
    - What type of support do you need from administration?
    - How can parents support your idea?
    - Are there community members or organizations that could share information or support your work?
    - Are there people within the school with existing connections who can help bring your idea to fruition?
• Student voice and input
    - What can you co-create with students to make your idea stronger?
    - What kind of input would you want or be able to get from students before implementing your new idea?
    - What type of feedback would you want in order to determine if the new idea worked for your students?

Wrapping It Up

Look through the comprehensive list in Figure 7.1. Start with celebrating the great things that are already happening in your classroom. Now go through the list again, focusing on the items that you marked as priorities and the places where you added notes in the "next steps" column.

- Are there areas that you already have ideas for? If so, that can be a great place to start.
- If, as you were reading, you realized that you felt something was missing from your classroom or from what your students are experiencing, that "something" can also be a place to dig in.
- Is there someone who came to mind to collaborate with on one of these ideas so that now you can't wait to get started? Then start there and share this book with that person.
- Are there barriers to implementation of your idea? How can you overcome those barriers?

This book certainly doesn't have all the answers for how to engage students in the middle grades, but I'm hoping that it gives you a starting point as you continue to think about your students, their experiences, and how to light the spark and keep the flame going. Figure 7.2 (see p. 172) invites you to answer some questions that can guide you along your path forward.

As I wrote this book and reflected on my own classroom, my former students, and the many educators that I have worked with over the last 25 years, I found myself in awe of the work that is done every day in schools throughout the country. I am incredibly grateful to everyone who is dedicated to working each day to help students to find their spark and make the conditions for learning engaging, relevant, and inspiring.

FIGURE 7.1
A Comprehensive Checklist of Things to Keep in Mind

Chapter	Is this part of my classroom environment or practices?	Yes/No/Unsure	Is this a priority for me right now?	Next steps
1	Opportunities for students to explore different identities or roles			
1	Opportunities for students to have new experiences			
1	Sharing the *why* behind what students are learning			
1	Students feeling like they belong			
1	Students feeling like their work is meaningful			
1	Every student having a trusted adult that they can go to			
1	Every student having something that sparks their learning and keeps them motivated			
2	Various levels of data that help inform instruction			

(continued)

FIGURE 7.1—(continued)

A Comprehensive Checklist of Things to Keep in Mind

Chapter	Is this part of my classroom environment or practices?	Yes/No/ Unsure	Is this a priority for me right now?	Next steps
2	Various levels of data that help inform the classroom environment			
2	Opportunities for students to share their thoughts about the classroom environment and practices			
2	Opportunities for students to reflect on their learning			
2	Opportunities to better understand how students are experiencing school			
2	Opportunities for open dialogue with students about data			
3	Opportunities for students to share their stories as part of the curriculum			

Chapter	Is this part of my classroom environment or practices?	Yes/No/Unsure	Is this a priority for me right now?	Next steps
3	Opportunities for students to share their stories to build community			
3	Opportunities for me to share my story with students			
3	Opportunities to share multiple perspectives through short stories, articles, children's books, and so on			
3	Opportunities for family members or other members of the community to share their stories			
3	Opportunities for students to learn and share their family's story			
4	Opportunities for arts-based activities			
4	Opportunities for play, collaboration, and competition			

(continued)

FIGURE 7.1—(continued)
A Comprehensive Checklist of Things to Keep in Mind

Chapter	Is this part of my classroom environment or practices?	Yes/No/Unsure	Is this a priority for me right now?	Next steps
4	Opportunities for students to express their emotions			
4	Opportunities for students to analyze different forms of art			
4	Opportunities for students to create different forms of art			
4	Opportunities for choice in how students express themselves			
4, 5	Opportunities for choice in how students show their learning			
5	Opportunities for students to engage in assignments that address intellectual need and emphasize process over product			
5	Opportunities for students to learn skills that are transferable to other areas of their life			

Chapter	Is this part of my classroom environment or practices?	Yes/No/Unsure	Is this a priority for me right now?	Next steps
5	Opportunities for students to make an impact in their community			
5	Opportunities for students to connect with people who are making an impact in the community			
6	Opportunities to create connections every day in my classroom			
7	Time to reflect on my classroom and how it connects to the middle school experience I want students to have			
7	Time to collaborate with others in my building and my community			
7	Support for my ideas from relevant stakeholders			

FIGURE 7.2

Finding the SPARK for the Path Forward

Study—This chapter includes a lot of reflection questions. What stood out for you as you reflected on your own middle school experience, the suggestions for getting started, and the checklist of key elements in the preceding chapters?

Pilot—Thinking about the suggestions at the end of this chapter, what did you identify as priorities? What is the first thing you will implement?

Analyze—How will you determine if the new things you try are working? What qualitative and quantitative data can you collect?

Reflect—If you tried something you never had done before, how did that experience feel? If you added something new, do you think it enhanced your existing lesson or unit? If you created a new idea for the future, what do you hope the outcome will be for your students?

Kindle—Considering the dreams you voiced at the beginning of the chapter as you reflected on your own experience and your hopes for your students, how are you going to make those a reality for you and for your students?

Acknowledgments

I would like to extend my heartfelt thanks to all of my former students for allowing me to learn alongside you and share in some amazing experiences along the way. This book literally couldn't have been written without you. Special thanks to those who lent their voices and expertise to this book, including Dennis, Joy, Kati, Jenna, Nahrin, and Nora.

To my current colleagues at the University of Chicago's To&Through Project and former colleagues at McCracken, Umoja, and Sullivan, I truly appreciate your brilliance and unwavering support throughout this journey. Whether offering advice on cover art and titles, sharing your own experiences in writing a book, or even just asking how the process was going, I am grateful to work with such incredible people every day and to be able to share even a small fraction of the work we have done together over the years. A special shout-out to Dave for the many walks we took where you helped me think through ideas and areas where I felt stuck.

Thank you also to all of the educators in the University of Chicago's To&Through Middle Grades Network. Your commitment to supporting middle school students inspires me every day and made me want write this book to share the amazing work that middle school educators do every single day.

And to Naomi, Jenny, Augie, Camille, Meredith, Dora, Cathy, Sarah, Curtis, Yekaterina, Brooklyn, and Ashlee, thank you for taking time out of your busy schedules to be interviewed and for sharing your stories and ideas. Your examples bring these chapters to life in such wonderful ways!

To my friends who listened to me and encouraged me along the way, I know if I try to list you all I will forget someone, so please know that I appreciate you all and am grateful for you.

Thank you also to Susan Hills and Liz Wegner from ASCD for your guidance throughout the process of writing my first book. Your advice, patience, and quick responses made this journey a smooth one. And to Tim, Rachel, Leticia, Mary, Lisa, and Abby, thank you for being the first readers of this book and for sharing your support.

And finally, to my family, I couldn't have done this without you. Especially to my mom and all the current and former educators in our family—education is the cornerstone of a democratic society, and I am grateful to stand with you in protecting it. To Molly and John, my very favorite former middle school students, thank you for sharing your experiences with me, both good and bad, and for helping me to be a better educator and mom along the way. Lastly, to you, Mike, your confidence, love, and support mean the world to me in this and all our endeavors over the years. I couldn't imagine doing this without you. I love you more.

References

Adichie, C. N. (2009, October 7). *The danger of a single story* [Video]. TED Global. https://www.ted.com/talks/chimamanda_ngozi_adichie_the_danger_of_a_single_story?subtitle=en

Barry, M. (n.d.). Interview for empathy. Stanford d.School. https://bplawassets.learningaccelerator.org/artifacts/pdf_files/d.school-Interview-for-Empathy.pdf

Benson, P. L. (2008). *Sparks: How parents can help ignite the hidden strengths of teenagers.* Jossey-Bass.

Bishop, R. S. (1990). Mirrors, windows, and sliding glass doors. *Perspectives: Choosing and Using Books for the Classroom, 6*(3), ix–xi.

Borton, T. (1970). *Reach, touch, and teach: Student concerns and process education.* McGraw-Hill.

Brown, B. (2018). *Dare to lead: Brave work. Tough conversations. Whole hearts.* Random House.

Chandler, C. (2017, January 15). The first 5 minutes: Ignite student learning. *MiddleWeb.* https://www.middleweb.com/33852/the-first-5-minutes-ignite-student-learning/

Collins, M., & Tamarkin, C. (1990). *Marva Collins' way: Updated.* Penguin.

De Carolis, B., D'Errico, F., & Rossano, V. (2021). Pepper as a storyteller: Exploring the effect of human vs. robot voice on children's emotional experience. In C. Ardito, R. Lanzilotti, A. Malizia, H. Petrie, A. Piccinno, G. Desolda, & K. Inkpen (Eds.), *Human-computer interaction—INTERACT 2021.* Springer, Cham. https://doi.org/10.1007/978-3-030-85616-8_27

Farrington, C. A., Maurer, J., McBride, M. R. A., Nagaoka, J., Puller, J. S., Shewfelt, S., Weiss, E. M., & Wright, L. (2019). *Arts education and social-emotional learning outcomes among K–12 students: Developing a theory of action* [Report]. Ingenuity and the University of Chicago Consortium on School Research.

Farrington, C. A., Roderick, M., Allensworth, E., Nagaoka, J., Keyes, T. S., Johnson, D. W., & Beechum, N. W. (2012a). *Teaching adolescents to become learners. The role of noncognitive factors in shaping school performance: A critical literature review* [Executive summary]. University of Chicago Consortium on School Research.

Farrington, C. A., Roderick, M., Allensworth, E., Nagaoka, J., Keyes, T. S., Johnson, D. W., & Beechum, N. W. (2012b). *Teaching adolescents to become learners. The role of noncognitive factors in shaping school performance: A critical literature review* [Report]. University of Chicago Consortium on School Research.

Fierstein, H. (2012, March 29). Reimagining the story of *Newsies*. *HuffPost*. https://www.huffpost.com/entry/newsies-broadway_b_1385817

Giedd, J. (2002). Inside the teenage brain [Interview]. *Frontline*. PBS. https://www.pbs.org/wgbh/pages/frontline/shows/teenbrain/interviews/giedd.html

Gripshover, S., Londerée, A., Ahuvia, I., Shyjka, A., Kroshinsky, F. S., Ryan, N., Farrington, C. A., & Paunesku, D. (2022). *Learning conditions are an actionable, early indicator of math learning*. PERTS. https://perts.net/research/early-indicators

Harel, G. (2008). A DNR perspective on mathematics curriculum and instruction, Part II. *Zentralblatt für Didaktik der Mathematik, 40*, 893–907.

Harper, R., Hermann, H., & Waite, W. (2018, August). *Science of adolescent learning: How body and brain development affect student learning*. Alliance for Excellent Education. https://all4ed.org/wp-content/uploads/2018/08/Science-of-Adolescent-Learning-How-Body-and-Brain-Development-Affect-Student-Learning.pdf

Harvard Graduate School of Education. (2024). *Relationship mapping strategy*. https://mcc.gse.harvard.edu/resources-for-educators/relationship-mapping-strategy

Learning for Justice. (n.d.). *Guiding principles*. https://www.learningforjustice.org/frameworks/teaching-the-civil-rights-movement/guiding-principles

Meyer, D. (2015, June 17). If math is the aspirin, then how do you create the headache? *dy/dan.* https://blog.mrmeyer.com/2015/if-math-is-the-aspirin-then-how-do-you-create-the-headache/

Nagaoka, J., Farrington, C. A., Ehrlich, S. B., & Heath, R. D. (2015, June). *Foundations for young adult success: A developmental framework.* University of Chicago Consortium on Chicago School Research. https://consortium.uchicago.edu/sites/default/files/2018-10/Foundations%20for%20Young%20Adult-Jun2015-Consortium.pdf

National Equity Project. (n.d.). Culturally responsive teaching. https://www.nationalequityproject.org/culturally-responsive-teaching

National Museum of African American History and Culture (n.d.). *The importance of visual art.* https://nmaahc.si.edu/explore/stories/importance-visual-art

The Nelson Mandela Foundation Archive at the Centre of Memory. (2003, July 16). *Item 909—Lighting your way to a better future: Speech delivered by Mr N R Mandela at launch of Mindset Network.* https://archive.nelsonmandela.org/index.php/za-com-mr-s-909

Paunesku, D., & Farrington, C. A. (2020). Measure learning environments, not just students, to support learning and development. *Teachers College Record, 112*(14), 1–26. https://doi.org/10.1177/016146812012201404

Peterson, L. (2017, November 14). *The science behind the art of storytelling.* Harvard Business Publishing. https://www.harvardbusiness.org/the-science-behind-the-art-of-storytelling/

Raney, B. L. (2019). *One trusted adult: How to build strong connections and healthy boundaries with young people.* Brooklyn Raney.

Rembert, K. (2023). *The antiracist English language arts classroom.* Routledge.

Rolfe, G., Freshwater, D., & Jasper, M. (2001). *Critical reflection for nursing and the helping professions: A user's guide.* Palgrave Macmillan.

Safir, S., & Dugan, J. (2021). *Street data: A next-generation model for equity, pedagogy, and school transformation.* Corwin.

Sapolsky, R. M. (2018). *Behave: The biology of humans at our best and worst.* Penguin Books.

Scahill, J. (Host). (2021, March 17). Hope is a discipline: Mariame Kaba on dismantling the carceral state [Audio podcast]. *The*

Intercept. https://theintercept.com/2021/03/17/intercepted-mariame-kaba-abolitionist-organizing/

Scales, P. C. (2010). Finding the student spark: Missed opportunities in school engagement. *Search Institute Insights & Evidence, 5*(1), 1–13.

Scales, P. C., Benson, P. L., & Roehlkepartain, E. C. (2010). Adolescent thriving: The role of sparks, relationships, and empowerment. *Journal of Youth and Adolescence, 40*(3), 263–277. https://doi.org/10.1007/s10964-010-9578-6

Scanlon, C. (2024, July 30). *Decoding adolescence: Understanding behavior as a function of adolescent development and psychological needs* [PowerPoint presentation]. To&Through Middle Grades Network Summer Institute, Chicago. https://toandthrough.uchicago.edu/middle-grades-network-improvement-community

Search Institute. (2020). *Developmental relationships framework.* https://searchinstitute.org/resources-hub/developmental-relationships-framework

Spear, L. P. (2013, February). Adolescent neurodevelopment. *Journal of Adolescent Development, 52*(2), S7–S13. https://doi.org/10.1016/j.jadohealth.2012.05.006

Spinks, S. (2000, March 9). Adolescent brains are works in progress. *Frontline.* PBS. https://www.pbs.org/wgbh/pages/frontline/shows/teenbrain/work/adolescent.html

Tambe, N. (2023, July 14). Top 20 skills that employers look for in candidates. *Forbes.* https://www.forbes.com/advisor/in/business/top-skills-to-get-a-job/

Woolliscroft, J. O. (2020). *Implementing biomedical innovations into health, education, and practice: Preparing tomorrow's physicians.* Academic Press.

Youth-Nex. (2023). *Portrait of a thriving youth* [Report]. University of Virginia School of Education and Human Development.

Zarkhosh, H. (2024, March 6). Nothing about us without us: Promoting disability history and awareness in classrooms. *Facing History & Ourselves.* https://www.facinghistory.org/ideas-week/nothing-about-us-without-us-promoting-disability-history-awareness-classrooms

Index

The letter *f* following a page locator denotes a figure.

Advice April, 145
amygdala, hijacking the, 8–9
armoring up, 25
art, integrating throughout the curriculum
  + understanding emotion, 151–152
  as an assessment, 103–107
  film, incorporating, 100–103
  hard topics, talking about, 88
  images, analyzing, 92–95
  learning stations, 107–111
  messy mural activity, 152
  music, incorporating, 97–100
  photographs, analyzing, 95–97
  power of, educate to realize, 88
  present, connecting to the, 88
  propaganda, analyzing, 89–92
  reasons for, 78–79
  resist simple storytelling, 89
  social-emotional learning and, 79–83
  unseen, revealing the, 88–89

arts
  emotion and, 79, 82–83
  Harlem Renaissance vignette, 77–78
  learning using the, 79–80
  making an impact with, learning how, 159–161
  power of, 88, 111–112
arts-based classrooms, 80–81, 83–87
arts integration + understanding emotion, 151–152
assessment, art as an, 103–107
assignments, late-work policies, 19–20
autonomy, developing, 121–125

background knowledge, creating a shared sense of, 59–60
beginning of year survey, 30–31*f*
behavior, developmental, 6–7
belonging in community, 9–10, 65
brain development
  in adolescence, 3–4, 6
  expectations and, 14

brain development—*(continued)*
    experiences for, 15
    noncognitive, 9–10
    stories in, 51–52

change, ideas for implementing, 167–171*f*
choice, giving students, 121–125
classrooms
    arts-based, 80–81, 83–87
    divisions in, 16
    implementing change, ideas for, 163–166, 167–171*f*
    play in, 81
    ways students can act and reflect in, 15*f*
classroom structure, 3–4
community
    belonging in, 9–10, 65
    building, 86
    stories from the, 61–64
connections, life and school, 114–121. *See also* life outside school
creative thinking, arts-based strategies for, 83–87
curiosity, 6–7
curriculum, integrating art throughout the
    as an assessment, 103–107
    film, incorporating, 100–103
    hard topics, talking about, 88
    images, analyzing, 92–95
    learning stations, 107–111
    music, incorporating, 97–100
    photographs, analyzing, 95–97
    power, educate to realize, 88
    present, connecting to the, 88
    propaganda, analyzing, 89–92

curriculum—*(continued)*
    resist simple storytelling, 89
    unseen, revealing the, 88–89
curriculum, storytelling throughout the, 59–61

data
    feeling safe with, 25–26
    levels of, 21–24
    for measurement vs. improvement, 24–25
    sharing with students, 43–48
    student data + storytelling + connections to life outside school, 147
data analysis
    data circles, 44–45
    4, 2, Q protocol, 43–44
    protocols for, 42
    reflection in, 46
    with students, 43–48
data circles, 44–45
data collection
    defensiveness, guarding against, 25–26
    empathy interviews, 33–37, 34*f*
    focus groups, 39–41
    K-W-L reflection tool for, 27–29, 27*f*
    meaningful, 21–22, 24
    qualitative data, 26–29, 27*f*
    student shadows, 37–39
    surveys, 29, 30–32*f*, 32–33
Data Dive December, 143–144

education in a changing world, 161–162

emotion
    arts and, 79, 82–83, 151–152
    play and, 81
    processing, 82
    understanding, + arts integration, 152
empathy interviews, 33–37, 34*f*
experiences, designing, 80–82

Facts and Figures Friday, 142–143
family history storytelling project. *See also* storytelling
    checklists and rubrics, 73–74
    families, communicating with, 71–72, 72*f*
    feedback component, 75–76
    overview, 66–68
    power of, 65, 76
    reflection in, 69–71
    sharing information, options for, 68–69, 74–75
    timelines, using, 73
    who to interview, 71
    writing a narrative, 68–69
family stories, 59–60, 62–63
film, incorporating, 100–103
Flair February, 144
focus groups, 39–41
forgetting curve, 14
4, 2, Q protocol, 43–44

hard topics, talking about, 88
hope, 156, 162, 163

identity, questions of, 2–3
identity formation
    + storytelling, 150–151
    domains of, 5

identity formation—(*continued*)
    exploration's role in, 5–6
    honoring student stories in, 53
    risk-taking in, 8
    why, questioning the, 6–8
images, analyzing, 92–95
independence, developing, 84–85
intellectual necessity, addressing, 118–119

Journaling January, 144
journals, dialogue, 59

K-W-L reflection tool, 27–29, 27*f*

late-work policies, 19–20
learning, multisensory landmarks for, 79–80
learning stations, 107–111
life outside school. *See also* service learning, interdisciplinary project
    + finding the why, 153–155
    a changing world, 161–162
    connecting to daily, 149
    experts, finding, 154
    giving students choice, 121–125
    letter-writing assignment, 158–159
    making connections, 114–121
    relevant skills, learning, 126–129
    share-outs, 153
    "Shine a Light" recording, 113–114

Making Meaning May, 145
map data, 22–23
March Madness, 144–145
Meaningful Monday, 142
messy mural activity, 152
middle school
    letter-writing assignment, 158–159
    making an impact, learning how, 159–161
    transitions, 156–157
mindsets affecting performance, 9
music, incorporating, 97–100

Necessity Principle, 119
Noticings November, 143

Options and Opportunities October, 143

performance, academic mindsets affecting, 9
photographs, analyzing, 95–97
pictures, sharing with, 49–50
play, incorporating, 81
possibility, incorporating, 82
power, educate to realize, 88
presence, incorporating, 81
present, connecting to the, 88
problem solving, arts-based strategies for, 83–87
project survey, 32*f*
propaganda, analyzing, 89–92
pulse checks, 54

quarterly survey, 31*f*
questioning, developmental, 6–7

question of the day, 54–55
questions
    check-in, 147–149
    in data analysis, 45

reflection
    in data analysis, 46
    in data collection, 27–29, 27*f*
    interdisciplinary service learning stage, 133, 134*f*, 135
relationships
    peer, 16
    trusting, developing, 10–13
relevancy, building, 115. *See also* service learning, interdisciplinary project
relevancy, storytelling to build, 60
relevant skills, learning, 126–129
risk reduction, 10
risk-taking, 5–6

safety, academic, 9
satellite data, 22
service learning, interdisciplinary project
    authentic audience, presenting to an, 137
    demonstration and celebration, 133
    evaluation, 135–136
    experts, talking to, 137
    investigation component, 131
    planning and preparation stage, 131–132
    reflection stage, 133, 134*f*, 135
    taking action, 132–133, 134*f*
    teacher's role in, 137

service learning, interdisciplinary project—(*continued*)
    timing, planning for, 136–137
service learning, interdisciplinary, reasons for, 129–130
share-outs, 153
"Shine a Light" recording, 113–114
skills, learning relevant, 126–129
social-emotional learning, arts integration and, 79–83
sparks
    of connection, creating daily and monthly, 141–146
    defined, 13
    fostering, methods, 13–14
    power of, xii
stories
    collective, building, 53
    community, bringing in, 61–64
    daily prompts to elicit, 54–55
    honoring student, 53
    from multiple perspectives, 150
    students sharing their, 150–151
    yourself in, 56–58
storytelling. *See also* family history storytelling project
    + identity formation, 150–151

storytelling—(*continued*)
    + student data + connections to life outside school, 147
    importance of, 50–52
    with pictures, 49–50
    resist simple, 89
    throughout the curriculum, 59–61
Storytelling September, 143
street data, 23–25
student data + storytelling + connections to life outside school, 147
student shadows, 37–39
success, belonging and, 65
surveys, 29, 30–32*f*, 32–33

Talented Tuesday, 142
Talkative Thursday, 142
team-building activities, 85
trust, 10–13, 84–87

unseen, revealing the, 88–89

why
    explaining the, 14–15
    finding the + connecting life outside school, 153–155
    questioning the, 6–8
Why Wednesday, 142
writing, narrative, 59

About the Author

Jennifer K. Ciok is an educator with more than 25 years of experience in the field. She served as a classroom teacher for 15 years and since then has been supporting teachers and leaders at a systems level on school culture, climate, and classroom learning conditions. As the manager of coaching and improvement for the University of Chicago's To&Through Middle Grades Network, Jennifer works closely with school teams to create more equitable and supportive educational environments where middle schoolers thrive. In this role, she supports middle grade educators in Chicago Public Schools to help build these systems using qualitative and quantitative data and research to define problems of practice and implement change ideas to better support students.

Jennifer has delivered professional development to hundreds of educators and serves on multiple boards, including her community's local school board. She has also been invited to write articles for various publications and speak on panels, on podcasts, and at national conferences. Her bachelor's and master's degrees are from Ohio University.

Related ASCD Resources

At the time of publication, the following resources were available (ASCD stock numbers in parentheses).

Amplify Student Voices: Equitable Practices to Build Confidence in the Classroom by AnnMarie Baines, Diana Medina, and Caitlin Healy (#122061)

Attack of the Teenage Brain! Understanding and Supporting the Weird and Wonderful Adolescent Learner by John Medina (#118024)

Differentiation in Middle and High School: Strategies to Engage All Learners by Kristina Doubet and Jessica Hockett (#115008)

From Stressed Out to Stress Wise: How You and Your Students Can Navigate Challenges and Nurture Vitality by Abby Wills, Anjali Deva, and Niki Saccareccia (#123004)

Improve Every Lesson Plan with SEL by Jeffrey Benson (#121057)

Math Fact Fluency: 60+ Games and Assessment Tools to Support Learning and Retention by Jennifer Bay-Williams and Gina Kling (#118014)

The Power of the Adolescent Brain: Strategies for Teaching Middle and High School Students by Thomas Armstrong (#116017)

The Relevant Classroom: Six Steps to Foster Real-World Learning by Eric Hardie (#120003)

Teach for Authentic Engagement by Lauren Porosoff (#123045)

Teaching Students to Communicate Mathematically by Laney Sammons (#118005)

Tell Your Story: Teaching Students to Become World-Changing Thinkers and Writers by Pam Allyn and Ernest Morrell (#122031)

Tomorrow's High School: Creating Student Pathways for Both College and Career by Gene Bottoms (#122017)

For up-to-date information about ASCD resources, go to www.ascd.org. You can search the complete archives of *Educational Leadership* at **www.ascd.org/el**. To contact us, send an email to member@ascd.org or call 1-800-933-2723 or 703-578-9600.

Transform Instruction to
Transform Students' Lives

Our Transformational Learning Principles (TLPs) are evidence-based practices that ensure students have access to high-impact, joyful learning experiences.

Endorsed by AASA and NASSP, the TLPs provide a shared language and a framework for reimagining teaching and learning, focusing on nurturing student growth, guiding intellectual curiosity, and empowering learners to take ownership of their education.

NURTURE · Connect Learning · Ensure Equity · Cultivate Belonging

GUIDE · Spark Curiosity · Develop Expertise · Elevate Reflection

EMPOWER · Prioritize Authentic Experiences · Ignite Agency

Transformational Learning Principles

The Meaningful Middle School Classroom relates to the **cultivate belonging** and **prioritize authentic experiences** principles.

Learn more at **ascd.org/tlps**

DON'T MISS A SINGLE ISSUE OF THIS AWARD-WINNING MAGAZINE.

iste+ascd
educational leadership

If you belong to a Professional Learning Community, you may be looking for a way to get your fellow educators' minds around a complex topic. Why not delve into a relevant theme issue of *Educational Leadership*, the journal written by educators for educators?

Subscribe now and browse or purchase back issues of our flagship publication at **www.ascd.org/el**. Discounts on bulk purchases are available.

iste+ascd

Arlington, VA USA
1-800-933-2723

www.ascd.org
www.iste.org

www.ingramcontent.com/pod-product-compliance
Lightning Source LLC
Chambersburg PA
CBHW070550010526
44118CB00012B/1277